Conversations with Don DeLillo

Literary Conversations Series
Peggy Whitman Prenshaw
General Editor

Photo credit: © 2004 Nancy Crampton

Conversations with Don DeLillo

Edited by Thomas DePietro

University Press of Mississippi
Jackson

Books by Don DeLillo

Americana. Boston: Houghton Mifflin, 1971.
End Zone. Boston: Houghton Mifflin, 1972.
Great Jones Street. Boston: Houghton Mifflin, 1973.
Ratner's Star. New York: Knopf, 1976.
Players. New York: Knopf, 1977.
Running Dog. New York: Knopf, 1978.
The Names. New York: Knopf, 1982.
White Noise. New York: Viking, 1985.
The Day Room. New York: Knopf, 1987.
Libra. New York: Viking, 1988.
Mao II. New York: Viking, 1991.
Underworld New York: Scribner, 1997.
Valparaiso. New York: Scribner, 1999.
The Body Artist. New York: Scribner, 2001.
Cosmopolis. New York: Scribner, 2003.

www.upress.state.ms.us

The University Press of Mississippi is a member of the Association of American University Presses.

13 12 11 10 09 08 07 06 05 4 3 2 1
♾
Library of Congress Cataloging-in-Publication Data

DeLillo, Don.
    Conversations with Don DeLillo / edited by Thomas DePietro.
        p. cm. — (Literary conversations series)
    Includes bibliographical references and index.
    ISBN 1-57806-703-0 (cloth : alk. paper) — ISBN 1-57806-704-9 (pbk. : alk. paper)
        1. DeLillo, Don—Interviews. 2. Novelists, American—20th century—Interviews.
    3. Fiction—Authorship. I. DePietro, Thomas. II. Title. III. Series.

PS3554.E4425Z465   2005
813'.54—dc22
    [B]   2004058839

British Library Cataloging-in-Publication Data available

Contents

Introduction

Don DeLillo's widely-performed play *Valparaiso* (1999) takes satirical aim at the motives of interviewers. An Oprah-like TV host asks a guest, "What are you hiding in your heart?" The man replies: "There's nothing I haven't openly spoken about. I've answered every question. I've answered some questions seventy, eighty, ninety times. I've answered in the same words every time. I do the same thoughtful pauses in the exact same places. We're dealing with the important things here." Given Don DeLillo's well-known aversion to discussing himself or his own work, it's easy to imagine that the media circus of *Valparaiso*, in which a simple confusion of place names turns a hapless businessman into an accidental celebrity, speaks to the author's own experiences on the firing line. As one interviewer in the play suggests, "Everything is the interview."

Valparaiso, coming on the heels of DeLillo's celebrated novel *Underworld* (1997), no doubt reflected its author's exhaustion after the most extensive publicity campaign of his career. But to read it autobiographically would be an oversimplification, since DeLillo's clever drama concerns much more than the absurdity of so-called reality television and the poetry found in the babble of airline announcements. And, besides, DeLillo's attitude towards the commerce of books and the relentlessness of interviewers hasn't changed over the years. As he remarked to a reporter from *The Washington Post*: "Interviewers want to feel that they're cracking a barrier that doesn't exist. I've been called 'reclusive' a hundred times and I'm not even remotely in that category. But people want to believe this because it satisfies some romantic conception of what a dedicated writer is and how he ought to live. 'I know you never do interviews.' They say that to me all the time. 'But here I am' is my stock reply."[1]

Sure enough, DeLillo has submitted himself to numerous interviewers from all sorts of magazines and journals, and the best, spanning some twenty years, are collected here. The most recent continue to claim that their subject is a "cipher," with a "cryptic air"; he's "enigmatic," "invisible," and "all business." Of course, DeLillo encourages some of these characterizations. When he emerged to accept his American Book Award for *White Noise* in 1985, he addressed the audience at the New York Public Library saying, "I'm sorry I couldn't be here tonight," and sat down.

To be sure, Don DeLillo is a private man who for most of his distinguished career has avoided the typical blandishments of success: no teaching, no writing conferences, no judges' panels. But since his first interview (Thomas LeClair) in 1982, DeLillo has been hiding in plain sight. He makes himself available when the occasion arises, and lately he has begun to read from his work in public. Television, though, continues to represent not just the kind of celebrity DeLillo spurns, but also the consumerist vision he so trenchantly explores in his fiction. The very first response in that first sit-down with LeClair becomes the theme for all future inquisitors. When LeClair asks why DeLillo offers so little biographical information on his dust jackets, he replies (paraphrasing one of his favorite authors, James Joyce): "Silence, exile, cunning, and so on. It's my nature to keep quiet about most things."

DeLillo talked to LeClair after having already published six novels to great critical acclaim, and he would submit to just one more interview (Harris, 1982) before the wider success of *White Noise* in 1985. The book that forced him further into the open is *Libra* (1988), his fact-based account of Lee Harvey Oswald and the assassination of President Kennedy (see, in particular, Arensberg, Connolly, Goldstein, and DeCurtis). Unlike E. L. Doctorow or Robert Coover, DeLillo felt compelled to make clear the distinctions between fact and fiction in the novel, to remain "faithful to what we know of history." Oswald, who appears in earlier (and later) DeLillo novels, remains for him a classic loner and outsider, part of the underground history of our times. In many interviews, DeLillo returns not just to his interpretation of these events, but to the elaborate research that went into his recreation of them: the hours poring over the complete Warren Report, the field trips to Dallas, and his own coincidental connection to Oswald (they both lived nearby in the Bronx at one point).

This concern with the "power of history" and the need to distinguish fact from fancy arise again with *Underworld*, a masterly and massive novel that also blends the real and imagined. As DeLillo tells his interviewers (Howard, Remnick, Echlin), it all began with some fortuitous research linking a famous baseball game and nuclear weapons. What some critics at the time didn't seem to realize is that many of the wilder events in the novel are true. (Yes, Frank Sinatra, J. Edgar Hoover, Toots Shor, and Jackie Gleason all attended together the famous Giants-Dodgers playoff game in 1951, to cite just one of these improbable facts). On the other hand, DeLillo tells us, he delighted in inventing the outrageous monologues he puts in the mouth of Lenny Bruce, one of the Cold War's underground prophets.

Underworld also found DeLillo in the "spirit of cooperation" with his publishers who, after all, had supposedly paid a huge sum for the novel. Money, promotional budgets, the business of books—DeLillo clearly has no interest in discussing these topics and prefers the old-fashioned notion that the writer writes, and the publisher sells. Numerous interviewers, especially those who came out of the woodwork with DeLillo's ascent into bestsellerdom with *Libra* and *Underworld*, strayed far from aesthetic questions. Suddenly, journalists wanted to know what he thought about all sorts of cultural and political matters. But despite his obvious interest in specific social and cultural events, DeLillo reminds his interviewers that he is after all a novelist, committed to the imagination and the voice of the individual. To their dismay, as well as to the delight of his few unsympathetic critics, DeLillo's characters do not speak for him. He sees his work as a mystery, born of a street-level love of language and a sensitivity to images.

Volumes in the Literary Conversations Series reprint interviews in their entirety in order to maintain their scholarly integrity, which leads to some inevitable repetition. In DeLillo's case, these repetitions are more prevalent simply because he often repeats himself and even quotes himself. Of course, he selects his words carefully, as one would expect of a novelist who makes language the very subject of his work. He stays on point at all times and controls the information about himself. As he told the *Washington Post*, "Once they start describing your house and your back yard, you're exposed in a curious way." The early interviews added little to the bare outline of DeLillo's life: date and place of birth, education, marriage. But over time, more facts of his life have emerged, and he has even reflected on some of their significance. His Catholic education, once simply noted by him, later explains his "failed" asceticism and his sense of the mystical. His Bronx, Italian-American background, which he barely discusses in early interviews, figures largely in the urban landscapes of *Underworld*, as it does in his sense of language and character. Hence, he refers to them more frequently in later profiles. Conversely, he argues that his experience as an advertising writer and his childhood reading explain little in his career. So, both remain non-starters throughout the interviews here.

DeLillo continually parries questions about literary and philosophical influences, even though his work seems to invoke an encyclopedia of intellectual and cultural history. A passing reference to reading Wittgenstein, and unsurprising acknowledgments of Joyce, Nabokov, Melville, and Pynchon are about all that DeLillo offers in this regard. The greater influences stem from purveyors of images: photographers, painters, and filmmakers. DeLillo refers time and again to his youthful encounters with New Wave cinema, especially Godard, and the abstract expressionist painters. The other much discussed influence is jazz, which, according to DeLillo, provided the musical background to his development as an artist; it's a music, after all, that celebrates individual expression, especially in the solo-driven post-bop of his youth.

Above all, DeLillo makes clear his greatest inspiration: New York City, whose streets he walks, whose subways he travels, whose inhabitants he overhears. The prescient social criticism in his novels derives not from some ideological agenda but from plain observation; DeLillo, despite what some of his adulatory critics suggest, is a realist, with the sensitivity of a recording angel and the craft of a consummate artist. Like many modern writers, DeLillo in his earlier interviews points us away from the teller to the tale. But over time, he explicates some of his intentions. If *Libra* required some explanation concerning its factuality, *Mao II* (1991) finds him explaining, among other things, its title, which comes from Andy Warhol's painting of Mao. As just another of his many celebrity portraits in the same silk-screened style, Warhol's *Mao* detaches itself from the historical record, which is exactly the sort of celebrity treatment DeLillo considers endemic to our time. It doesn't matter what you've achieved (or how many you've killed), you're a star.

As DeLillo makes clear in a number of interviews, *Mao II* also proposes some challenging ideas about the role of the novelist in our hype-driven culture. In words that seem prophetic (or irresponsible, depending on your point of view), DeLillo argues that novelists in our day have been supplanted by terrorists, as individuals who can alter our consciousness. Which is not to say that the novel has become irrelevant (or that we should become terrorists). What DeLillo means is that the terrorist captures our attention in a way that writers once did, that nonfictional documents, news reports, and photos, endlessly repeated on television, are at once potent and then sapped of their meaning.

Not an idle chatterer by any stretch of the imagination, DeLillo nevertheless comes alive with his favorite subject: baseball. In one of the most enjoyable interviews collected here, David Firestone of the *New York Times* had the clever idea to ask DeLillo about Mark McGwire's record-breaking home-run in 1998. While he admired McGwire's homage to Roger Maris (whose record he broke), DeLillo feared, not surprisingly, the endless repetition of the historic moment on television—a feature of modern media that continues to form the center of his critique.

A number of interviews focus on DeLillo's less-heralded work in the theater, work that forces him out of his solitary life as a novelist and into the collaborative world of the stage. As a writer of fiction in total control of his language, the experience of theatrical revision seems to come as a welcome alternative, and DeLillo's plays demonstrate a profound theatricality as a result. The three-dimensionality of the stage steers him away from psychological portraiture. Dialogue exists as it's filtered through an actor's voice. All of which no doubt offers a brave new world to this quintessential loner, a writer who tells many interviewers about his daily routine and the amount of time he spends staring quietly out his window. Theatrical productions always find DeLillo willing to talk, and what he has to say, whether it's about *The Day Room* or *Valparaiso*, or *The Mystery at the Middle of Ordinary Life*, is essentially the same: that DeLillo picks his genres by instinct, not design. Much in the way that the language of his books changes with each subject, his plays allow him to explore the mysteries of identity, since the characters change with each performance. Samuel Beckett of course is the prevailing spirit here, and he also once put off interviewers with the simple remark that he had "no views to inter."

DeLillo time and again rehearses his work habits—the hours at his desk punctuated by a midday run—and his devotion to his manual typewriter. The latter has actually grown in significance as he considers its influence on his composition, the shape of the words on the page, and the sounds they invoke. Many interviewers probe DeLillo for the secrets to his artistic triumph, but he is remarkably straightforward in response. Some journalists (not included here), especially after his greater fame with *Underworld*, load for bear, and try to take him down with snide remarks about his reticence. Or worse, they quote unfavorable reviews to him. DeLillo, always the gentleman, deflects these inquisitors with his typical aplomb, dismissing one with the apposite remark: "We've run out of conversation, haven't we?" So expect little of gossip value in these seventeen interviews: no rivalries are revealed, no axes ground. Just honest conversation from a very private man, an Italian-American after all who adheres to the old tribal notion of *omerta*—the code of silence that gains new significance when re-imagined by an artist struggling with the contradictions of self-expression.[2]

I want to thank, first of all, Dorothy Heyl, whose support means everything. Others who've provided topnotch assistance: Regina DePietro, Bill Hessberg, Mindi Hockenberry, and Neil Montone. This book makes no sense without Don DeLillo himself, whose words these mostly are.

TD

Notes
1. David Streitfeld. "Don DeLillo's Gloomy Muse," *Washington Post*, 14 May 1992, p. C-1.
2. Of great help to all DeLillo scholars and readers are two well-maintained web-sites: The Don DeLillo Society site, edited by Philip Nel; and *Don DeLillo's America*, run by Curt Gardner.

Chronology

1936   November 20th, born in the Bronx, New York, near Arthur Avenue, a largely Italian-American neighborhood.

1954   Graduated from Cardinal Hayes High School, a Catholic boys school in the Bronx.

1958   Attains B.A. in communication arts from Fordham University, also in the Bronx.

1959   Works as copywriter for Ogilvy & Mather.

1960   Publishes first story, "The River Jordan," in *Epoch*, the literary magazine at Cornell University.

1962   "Take the 'A' Train" appears in *Epoch*, and other stories appear throughout the decade in *The Kenyon Review* and *The Carolina Quarterly*.

1971   First novel, *Americana*, appears as well as his first story in *Esquire*.

1972   Publishes *End Zone* and in *Sports Illustrated*.

1973   *Great Jones Street* solidifies his reputation among critics.

1975   Marries Barbara Bennett, from Texas, a banker who eventually becomes a landscape designer.

1976   Publishes *Ratner's Star*.

1977   *Players* appears.

1978   Publishes *Running Dog*.

1979   First play appears in literary magazine, and he receives Guggenheim fellowship, which allows him to travel to Greece.

1980   *Amazons*, a fictional memoir of the first female professional hockey player, appears under the pseudonym "Cleo Birdwell."

1982   Publishes *The Names* and moves to the suburbs of New York City.

1983   Contributes an essay on the assassination of John Kennedy to *Rolling Stone*.

1984   Receives Award in Literature from the American Academy of Arts and Letters.

Conversations with Don DeLillo

An Interview with Don DeLillo

Thomas LeClair / 1982

From *Contemporary Literature*, 23, no. 1, pp. 19–31. © 1982. Reprinted by permission of the University of Wisconsin Press.

Of American novelists who began publishing in the '70s, Don DeLillo is one of the most prolific. He is also one of the most elusive. While his novels are located in America's fascinations—entertainment, big-time sport, intrigue—they are written with a detachment that causes reviewers to praise him for very different, sometimes contradictory intentions. The books are elusive because, for DeLillo, fiction draws its power from and moves toward mystery. Elusive, too, because DeLillo has not joined the literary auxiliary: he does not sit on panels, appear on television, judge contests, review books, or teach creative writing. He travels and writes.

DeLillo agreed to do this interview from what he thought was the safe distance of Greece. When I managed to get to Athens in September, 1979, and not long after I met him, he handed me a business card engraved with his name and "I don't want to talk about it." He does not like to discuss his work, but he is a witty conversationalist, an informed and generous guide, invaluable in Greek taxis and restaurants. At forty-three, DeLillo in his jeans and sneakers has the look of a just-retired athlete. He walks Athens' crowded streets like a linebacker, on his toes, eyes shifting, watching for crazed drivers among the merely reckless. When we taped in his apartment near Mt. Lycabetus, he spoke quietly and slowly, in a slight New York accent, searching for the precision he insists upon in his fiction. One soon understands from his uninflected tone, which sounds more like thought than talk, and from the silences between his short declarative sentences that Don DeLillo's elusiveness comes naturally, necessarily, from his concern with what he quotes Hermann Broch as calling "the word beyond speech."

DeLillo's books offer a precise and thorough anthropology of the present, an account of our kinship in myths, media, and conspiracies. His first novel, *Americana* (1971), begins in the television industry and moves cross country searching for relief from the image. The heroes of *End Zone* (1972) and *Great Jones Street* (1973) are football and rock stars trying to work free of their public mythologies. In *Players* (1977) and *Running Dog* (1978), DeLillo writes about up-to-date conspiracies prompted by the appeal of terrorism and pornography. The book DeLillo considers his best is *Ratner's Star* (1976), where he combines elements of children's literature, science fiction, and mathematics to create a conceptual monster. Like his more realistic fictions, *Ratner's Star* uses its bulk and abstraction to imply all that cannot be spoken in characters, words, and numbers.

—*Tom LeClair*

LeClair: Why do reference books give only your date of birth and the publication dates of your books?
DeLillo: Silence, exile, cunning, and so on. It's my nature to keep quiet about most things. Even the ideas in my work. When you try to unravel something you've written, you belittle it in a way. It was created as a mystery, in part. Here is a new map of the world; it is seven shades of blue. If you're able to be straightforward and penetrating about this invention of yours, it's almost as though you're saying it wasn't altogether necessary. The sources weren't deep enough. Maybe this view is overrefined and too personal. But I think it helps explain why some writers are unable or unwilling to discuss their work. There's an element of tampering. And there's a crossover that can be difficult to make. What you write, what you say about it. The vocabularies don't match. It's hard to correspond to reality, to talk sensibly about an idea or a theme that originates in a writer's desire to restructure reality.

But here I am, talking.

LeClair: Of your six novels, which one is closest to your own experience?
DeLillo: *Americana*, probably, in the sense that I drew material more directly from people and situations I knew firsthand. I was hurling things at the page. At the time I lived in a small apartment with no stove and the refrigerator in the bathroom and I thought first novels written under these circumstances ought to be novels in which great chunks of experience are hurled at the page. So that's what I did. The original manuscript was higher than my radio.

It's not an autobiographical novel. But I did use many things I'd seen, heard, knew about.

LeClair: Your work seems to me quite different in tone and in language from most contemporary fiction. I wondered if you felt that you were onto something different.

DeLillo: When I was about halfway through *Americana*, which took roughly four years to do, it occurred to me almost in a flash that I was a writer. Whatever tentativeness I'd felt about the book dropped away. I finished it in a spirit of getting a difficult, unwieldy thing out of the way, in a spirit of having proved certain things to myself. With *End Zone* I felt I was doing something easier and looser. I was working closer to my instincts. I paced things differently. Balances became important, starts and stops. I approached certain things from unusual angles, I think. Some of the characters have a made-up nature. They are pieces of jargon. They engage in wars of jargon with each other. There is a mechanical element, a kind of fragmented self-consciousness. I took this further in *Ratner's Star*, where characters don't just open their mouths to say hello. They have to make the action part of the remark. "My mouth says hello." "My ears hear." The characters are words on paper. This isn't necessarily true of the other books. *End Zone* and *Ratner's Star* are books of games, books in which fiction itself is a sort of game.

My work also grew more precise. I began to study things more, disassemble them. Possibly what I was studying was ways to use the language. It may be the case that with *End Zone* I began to suspect that language was a subject as well as an instrument in my work, although I'd find it hard to say in what ways exactly.

LeClair: Games are important in your fiction. Were they an early interest?

DeLillo: The games I've written about have more to do with rules and boundaries than with the freewheeling street games I played when I was growing up. People whose lives are not clearly shaped or marked off may feel a deep need for rules of some kind. People leading lives of almost total freedom and possibility may secretly crave rules and boundaries, some kind of control in their lives. Most games are carefully structured. They satisfy a sense of order and they even have an element of dignity about them. In *Ratner's Star* someone says, "Strict rules add dignity to a game." There are many games in *Ratner's Star*, and the book is full of adults acting like children—which is another reason why people play games, of course.

In *Running Dog*, Selvy is playing a game when he leads his pursuers in a straight line to southwest Texas, where he knows they'll try to kill him. In *End*

Zone, one of the games is football. There are others. Games provide a frame in which we can try to be perfect. Within sixty-minute limits or one-hundred-yard limits or the limits of a game board, we can look for perfect moments or perfect structures. In my fiction I think this search sometimes turns out to be a cruel delusion.

In *Players*, the rules become almost metaphysical. They involve inner restrictions. There's some of that in *Running Dog* as well. Empty landscapes seem to inspire games.

LeClair: Your third novel, *Great Jones Street*, is set in the empty landscape of its title. How did you happen to write about a rock star?
DeLillo: It's a game at the far edge. It's an extreme situation. I think rock is a music of loneliness and isolation. The Doors work very well at the beginning of the film *Apocalypse Now*. A man with a half-shattered mind, alone in a rented room. Noise, electricity, excess, Vietnam—all these things are tied together in *Great Jones Street*, and a certain tension is drawn out of the hero's silence, his withdrawal. Bucky Wunderlick's music moves from political involvement to extreme self-awareness to childlike babbling.

LeClair: Perhaps because of the game element, reviewers of your fiction have a hard time locating your attitudes toward your characters.
DeLillo: My attitudes aren't directed toward characters at all. I don't feel sympathetic toward some characters, unsympathetic toward others. I don't love some characters, feel contempt for others. They have attitudes; I don't.

Some people may have felt I disliked Pammy and Lyle in *Players*. Not true. I think these two characters are more typical of contemporary Americans than people want to believe. Lyle is an intelligent, high-strung, spiritually undernourished person. Pammy is more humane. She is also more prone to be affected by the shallow ideas drifting through her world, and she is constantly afraid. I can talk about them this way, but I can't talk about them as people I love or hate. They're people I recognize.

What writing means to me is trying to make interesting, clear, beautiful language. Working at sentences and rhythms is probably the most satisfying thing I do as a writer. I think after a while a writer can begin to know himself through his language. He sees someone or something reflected back at him from these constructions. Over the years it's possible for a writer to shape himself as a human being through the language he uses. I think written language, fiction, goes that deep. He not only sees himself but begins to make himself or remake himself. Of course, this is mysterious and subjective territory.

Writing also means trying to advance the art. Fiction hasn't quite been filled in or done in or worked out. We make our small leaps. This is the reason for the introduction to *Players*. All the main characters, seven of them, are introduced in an abstract way. They don't have names. Their connections to each other are not clear in all cases. They're on an airplane, watching a movie, but all the other seats are empty. They're isolated, above the story, waiting to be named. It's a kind of model-building. It's the novel in miniature. We can call it pure fiction in the sense that the characters have been momentarily separated from the storytelling apparatus. They're still ideas, vague shapes.

LeClair: What do you think of the renewed interest in "moral fiction"? Anthony Burgess wrote that the term "evil" has no meaning in *Running Dog*. Another reviewer complained that the book was reductive.

DeLillo: Moll Robbins is the weathervane for all the avarice in the book, the maneuverings for power. Her own imperfections may frustrate the reader who is looking for a moral center. The evil, or whatever we call it, is there. We can't position these acts and attitudes around a nineteenth-century heroine. They float in a particular social and cultural medium. A modern American medium. Half-heartedness and indifference are very much to the point. People tend to walk away from their own conspiracies. Hitler is a fatigued and defeated man dressed up like Charlie Chaplin.

I'd say the style and language reflect the landscape more than they reflect the writer's state of mind. The bareness is really the bareness and starkness of lower Manhattan and southwest Texas. And since the book is essentially a thriller, I felt the prose should be pared down. But the reductiveness belongs to character and setting, not to the author's view of things. The author was amused, by and large. The author thought most of the characters were damned funny.

Glen Selvy, who was not one of the funny ones, believes that choice is a subtle form of disease. He feels he has to commit what is in effect a ritual suicide. He is leaving behind whatever is difficult about life, whatever is complicated. I try to understand what makes Selvy go. I don't patronize him or feel contempt for him because he leads a life that is simplified to an extreme degree. Selvy feels that knowing his weapons, how to take them apart and put them back together, is a form of self-respect. He finds his truth in violence. He is an adept of violence, a semi-mystic.

LeClair: Is this the case with many of your main characters? They withdraw, reduce their relations, empty out, discipline themselves.
DeLillo: I think they see freedom and possibility as being too remote from what they perceive existence to mean. They feel instinctively that there's a certain struggle, a solitude they have to confront. The landscape is silent, whether it's a desert, a small room, a hole in the ground. The voice you have to answer is your own voice. In *End Zone*, Gary Harkness stops eating and drinking in the last paragraph. He goes on a hunger strike. He isn't protesting anything or reacting to anything specific. He is paring things down. He is struggling, trying to face something he felt had to be faced. Something nameless. I thought this was interesting. I couldn't give a name to it. He just stops eating. He refuses to eat.

LeClair: In *End Zone* you have a character taking a college course in "the untellable." That's not entirely facetious, is it?
DeLillo: I do wonder if there is something we haven't come across. Is there another, clearer language? Will we speak it and hear it when we die? Did we know it before we were born? If there are life forms in other galaxies, how do they communicate? What do they sound like?

The "untellable" points to the limitations of language. Is there something we haven't discovered about speech? Is there more? Maybe this is why there's so much babbling in my books. Babbling can be frustrated speech, or it can be a purer form, an alternate speech. I wrote a short story that ends with two babies babbling at each other in a car. This was something I'd seen and heard, and it was a dazzling and unforgettable scene. I felt these babies *knew* something. They were talking, they were listening, they were *commenting*, and above and beyond it all they were taking an immense pleasure in the exchange.

Glossolalia is interesting because it suggests there's another way to speak, there's a very different language lurking somewhere in the brain.

LeClair: Are you interested in specialized language?
DeLillo: Specialized languages can be very beautiful. Mysterious and precise at the same time. In *Ratner's Star* there's a dictionary definition of the word "cosine" that illustrates this, I think. Mathematics and astronomy are full of beautiful nomenclature. Science in general has given us a new language to draw from. Some writers shrink from this. Science is guilty; the language of science is tainted by horror and destruction. To me, science is a source of new names, new connections between people and the world. Rilke said we had to rename the world. Renaming suggests an innocence and a rebirth. Some words adapt, and these are the ones we use in our new world.

Then there is jargon, which I associate with television for some reason. The one was invented to deliver the other. But I'm interested in the way people talk, jargon or not. The original idea for *Players* was based on what could be called the intimacy of language. What people who live together really sound like. Pammy and Lyle were to address each other in the private language they'd constructed over years of living together. Unfinished sentences, childlike babbling, animal noises, foreign accents, ethnic dialects, mimicry, all of that. It's as though language is something we wear. The more we know someone, the easier it is to undress, to become childlike. But the idea got sidetracked, and only fragments survive in the finished book.

LeClair: Would you name some writers with whom you have affinities?
DeLillo: This is the great bar mitzvah question. Probably the movies of Jean-Luc Godard had a more immediate effect on my early work than anything I'd ever read. Movies in general may be the not-so-hidden influence on a lot of modern writing, although the attraction has waned, I think. The strong image, the short ambiguous scene, the dream sense of some movies, the artificiality, the arbitrary choices of some directors, the cutting and editing. The power of images. This is something I kept thinking about when I was writing *Americana*. This power had another effect. It caused people to walk around all day saying, "Movies can do *so much.*" It's movies in part that seduced people into thinking the novel was dead. The power of the film image seemed to be overwhelming our little world of print. Film could do so much. Print could only trot across the page. But movies and novels are too closely related to work according to shifting proportions. If the novel dies, movies will die with it.

The books I remember and come back to seem to be ones that demonstrate the possibilities of fiction. *Pale Fire, Ulysses, The Death of Virgil, Under the Volcano, The Sound and the Fury*—these come to mind. There's a drive and a daring that go beyond technical invention. I think it's right to call it a life-drive even though these books deal at times very directly with death. No optimism, no pessimism. No homesickness for lost values or for the way fiction used to be written. These books open out onto some larger mystery. I don't know what to call it. Maybe Hermann Broch would call it "the word beyond speech."

LeClair: There's an allusion to Wittgenstein in *End Zone*. Do you find something important in his work?
DeLillo: I've read parts of the *Tractatus*, but I have no formal training in mathematical logic and I couldn't say a thing about the technical aspects of the book. I like the way he uses the language. Even in translation, it's very evocative. It's like reading Martian. The language is mysteriously simple and self-assured. It suggests without the slightest arrogance that there's no alternative to these remarks. The statements are machine tooled. Wittgenstein is the language of outer space, a very precise race of people.

LeClair: There are references to Zen in most of your books. Would you consider it an influence on your work?
DeLillo: I may have used the word several times, but I think only in *Americana* is there any kind of extended reference, and it has more to do with people playing at Eastern religion than anything else. I know very little about Zen. I'm interested in religion as a discipline and a spectacle, as something that drives people to extreme behavior. Noble, violent, depressing, beautiful. Being raised as a Catholic was interesting because the ritual had elements of art to it and it prompted feelings that art sometimes draws out of us. I think I reacted to it the way I react today to theater. Sometimes it was awesome; sometimes it was funny. High funeral masses were a little of both, and they're among my warmest childhood memories.

LeClair: Are you interested in mathematics for the same reasons?
DeLillo: I started reading mathematics because I wanted a fresh view of the world. I wanted to immerse myself in something as remote as possible from my own interests and my own work. I became fascinated and ended up

writing a novel and then a play about mathematicians. Aside from everything else, pure mathematics is a kind of secret knowledge. It's carried on almost totally outside the main currents of thought. It's a language almost no one speaks. In *Ratner's Star* I tried to weave this secret life of mankind into the action of the book in the form of a history of mathematics, a cult history, the names of the leaders kept secret until the second half of the book, the mirror image, when the names appear in reverse order. This purest of sciences brings out a religious feeling in people. Numbers in particular have always had a mystical appeal. Numbers work in such surprising ways it's hard not to feel a sense of mystery and wonder.

LeClair: Do you consider *Ratner's Star* to be your best book?
DeLillo: We're supposed to say the one I'm doing now is my best book. Otherwise, *Ratner's Star*, yes.

LeClair: What were some of the influences on and intentions of *Ratner's Star*?
DeLillo: There's a structural model, the Alice books of Lewis Carroll. The headings of the two parts—"Adventures" and "Reflections"—refer to *Alice's Adventures in Wonderland* and *Through the Looking Glass*. The connection, as I say, is structural. It involves format, not characters or themes or story except in the loosest sense. It works from the particular to the general. What is real in *Alice* becomes an abstraction in *Ratner's Star*. The rabbit hole of Chapter One, for instance, becomes "substratum"—early or underground mathematics. There is also a kind of guiding spirit. This is Pythagoras. The mathematician-mystic. The whole book is informed by this link or opposition, however you see it, and the characters keep bouncing between science and superstition.

I was trying to produce a book that would be naked structure. The structure would be the book and vice versa. I wanted the book to become what it was about. Abstract structures and connective patterns. A piece of mathematics, in short. To do this I felt I had to reduce the importance of people. The people had to play a role subservient to pattern, form, and so on. This is difficult, of course, for all concerned, but I believed I was doing something new and was willing to take the risk. A book that is really all outline. My notes for the book interest me almost as much as the book does. This is an incriminating remark, but there you are.

I hadn't started out to do this. All I had in mind was a fourteen-year-old mathematical genius who is asked to decipher a message from outer space. Things started happening to this simple idea. Connections led to other connections. I began to find things I didn't know I was looking for. Mathematics led to science fiction. Logic led to babbling. Language led to games. Games led to mathematics. When I discovered uncanny links to Alice and *her* world, I decided I had to follow. Down the rabbit hole.

A friend of mine said it was like reading the first half of one book and the second half of a completely different book. It's true in a way. There's a strong demarcation between the parts. They are opposites. Adventures, reflections. Positive, negative. Discrete, continuous. Day, night. Left brain, right brain. But they also link together. The second part bends back to the first. Somebody ought to make a list of books that seem to bend back on themselves. I think Malcolm Lowry saw *Under the Volcano* as a wheel-like structure. And in *Finnegans Wake* we're meant to go from the last page to the first. In different ways I've done this myself. *Great Jones Street* bends back on itself in the sense that the book is the narrator's way of resurfacing. *Players* begins in darkness with an unidentified voice talking about motels. This is Lyle's voice, and the book ends with Lyle in a motel room in Canada, in blinding light. In *Ratner's Star*, Softly, who is a sort of white rabbit figure, leads Billy into the hole that will take him back to the beginning of the book. In Chapter One Billy had a bandage on his finger—the finger he cut near the end of the book.

LeClair: In *Ratner's Star*, in a much-quoted passage, you refer to a class of writers who write "crazed prose" and books that are not meant to be read. Is *Ratner's Star* in that category?
DeLillo: No it isn't, although I think I felt some of the pull of crazed prose. There's an element of contempt for meanings. You want to write outside the usual framework. You want to dare readers to make a commitment you know they can't make. That's part of it. There's also the sense of drowning in information and in the mass awareness of things. Everybody seems to know everything. Subjects surface and are totally exhausted in a matter of days or weeks, totally played out by the publishing industry and the broadcast industry. Nothing is too arcane to escape the treatment, the process. Making things difficult for the reader is less an attack on the reader than it is on the age and its facile knowledge-market. The writer is driven by his conviction that some

truths aren't arrived at so easily, that life is still full of mystery, that it might be better for you, Dear Reader, if you went back to the Living section of your newspaper because this is the dying section and you don't really want to be here. This writer is working against the age and so he feels some satisfaction at not being widely read. He is diminished by an audience.

LeClair: Do you think about your readers?

DeLillo: I don't have a sense of a so-called ideal reader and certainly not of a readership, that terrific entity. I write for the page. My mail tells me nothing useful about what might be out there in the way of readers. It comes in driblets, much of it from crazy people.

LeClair: Do you think they feel they have a sympathetic correspondent? There are crazy people in the backgrounds of your books.

DeLillo: Yes, they've crept in. The streets are full of disturbed people. For a long time I wondered where they were coming from, so many, at once. We now learn they've been let out of asylums and hospitals and into halfway houses and welfare hotels. I've always thought New York was a medieval city and this is another sign of that. They speak a kind of broken language. It's part of the language of cities, really. In *Players* these people are always talking to Pammy. They talk to Diana in *The Engineer of Moonlight*. In the subway arcades under Fourteenth Street you hear mostly Spanish and black English with bits of Yiddish, German, Italian, and Chinese, and then there's this strange broken language. The language of the insane is stronger than all the others. It's the language of the self, the pain of self.

LeClair: Is obsession necessary to create fiction that's better than pedestrian?

DeLillo: Obsession is interesting to writers because it involves a centering and a narrowing down, an intense convergence. An obsessed person is an automatic piece of fiction. He has a purity of movement, an integrity. There is a kind of sheen about him. To a writer, an obsessed person is *right there*. He is already on the page.

When it comes to writers being obsessed, I have one notion. Obsession as a state seems so close to the natural condition of a novelist at work on a book that there may be nothing else to say about it. It's not possible to say whether an obsession can drive someone to do better work. He's probably not obsessed. If he is obsessed, it's probably beside the point.

LeClair: How do you prepare to write?

DeLillo: By doing nothing. Keeping life simple. Giving ideas time to sort themselves out. I try to be patient. Time usually does the selecting for me. What I'm left with at the end of a given period is usually what I need to begin.

LeClair: What about the actual mechanics?

DeLillo: In the beginning I work brief shifts. The important mechanics are mental. A lot of mental testing goes on. Promising threads develop out of certain ideas or characters, and some of these lines reach almost to the end of the book, or out into infinity, since the book doesn't have anything resembling an end at this point. Other lines are very short. Again, most of this is mental. It's stored. Some things I'll take right to the machine. Writing is intense concentration, and the typewriter can act as a focusing tool or memory tool. It enables me to bore in on something more strongly. It also enables me to see the words being formed. What the words look like is important. How they look in combination. I have to see the words.

Past the early stages I work longer periods. I find myself nearing the end of certain early lines of thought. This represents progress. It reminds me that the work doesn't actually go out into infinity. These identical, shapeless, satisfying days will come to an end somewhere down the line.

LeClair: There's some very abstract spatial analysis of characters or situations in your fiction. Would you comment on its function?

DeLillo: It's a way to take psychology out of a character's mind and into the room he occupies. I try to examine psychological states by looking at people in rooms, objects in rooms. It's a way of saying we can know something important about a character by the way he sees himself in relation to objects. People in rooms have always seemed important to me. I don't know why or ask myself why, but sometimes I feel I'm *painting* a character in a room, and the most important thing I can do is set him up in relation to objects, shadows, angles.

LeClair: Does place have any effect on your composition?

DeLillo: Sometimes things insinuate themselves onto the page. When I was working on *Great Jones Street*, there was dynamiting going on all the time, and eventually these construction noises turned up in the book. But place has more important meanings. So much modern fiction is located precisely nowhere. This is Beckett and Kafka insinuating themselves onto the page. Their work is so woven into the material of modern life that it's not surprising so many writers choose to live there, or choose to have their characters live there. Fiction without a sense of real place is automatically a fiction of estrangement, and of course this is the point. As theory it has its attractions, but I can't write that way myself. I'm too interested in what real places look like and what names they have. Place is color and texture. It's tied up with memory and roots and pigments and rough surfaces and language, too. I'm interested in what mathematicians say. No matter how pure their work is, it has to be responsive to the real world, one way or another, in order to keep its vitality and to cleanse itself of effeteness and self-absorption.

LeClair: Would you comment on your play *The Engineer of Moonlight*? It seems to be a distillation of many of the ideas and voices in your fiction.
DeLillo: We talked earlier about people in rooms. The play is just that. People talking, people silent, people motionless, people juxtaposed with objects. There are four characters. What connects them is the awesome power of their loving. The main character is Eric Lighter, a once-great mathematician who is now a pathetic but compelling ruin. If the play has a line of development at all, it hinges on whether Eric's former wife will abandon a recent marriage and successful career to help the others transcribe and type Eric's half-insane memoirs, along with other day-to-day chores and obligations. The idea is absurd on the face of it. Diana ridicules the notion. Toward the end of the play she leaves the stage still denying that she'll stay. But we know she still feels a powerful love for Eric, for the aura of greatness that clings to him, and we feel uncertain about taking her at her word. The suggestion that she may stay is contained in a strange board game she'd played with the others earlier in Act Two. A game involving words and logic used in unfamiliar ways. If we take this game as a play within the play, what we see is that Diana, who has never played before, gradually comes to understand the strange and complex nature of the game—an understanding the audience doesn't share. Toward the end she is elated; she is saying it all begins to fit, the colors, the shapes, the names. She wants to play.

A Talk with Don DeLillo

Robert Harris / 1982

From *The New York Times Book Review*, October 10, 1982, p. 26. © 1982, *The New York Times*. Reprinted by permission of Robert Harris.

During the last 11 years Don DeLillo has published seven novels of wit and intelligence. He has examined advertising (*Americana*, 1971), football (*End Zone*, 1972), the rock music scene (*Great Jones Street*, 1973), science and mathematics (*Ratner's Star*, 1976), terrorism (*Players*, 1977), the conventional espionage thriller (*Running Dog*, 1978) and, in his new novel, *The Names*, Americans living abroad.

Yet despite his unusual versatility and inventiveness, it seems that relatively few readers other than the critics clamor for Mr. DeLillo's work. He is able to earn a living from his writing, but he has not had a large commercial success.

"I don't know what happens out there," he says. "I don't know how the machinery works or what curious chemical change has to take place before that sort of thing happens. I wouldn't speculate. I've always tried to maintain a certain detachment. I put everything into the book and very little into what happens after I've finished it."

Mr. DeLillo lives with his wife on a modest residential street in a suburb of New York City. One recent afternoon, Mr. DeLillo sat in his living room wearing a plaid shirt, blue jeans and moccasins, and discussed his past and present concerns as a writer.

Born in the Bronx in 1936, Mr. DeLillo attended Fordham University, where, he says, "the Jesuits taught me to be a failed ascetic." He hated school but readily reels off a list of early influences. "I think New York itself was an enormous influence," he says. "The paintings in the Museum of Modern Art, the music at the Jazz Gallery and the Village Vanguard, the movies of Fellini and Godard and Howard Hawks. And there was a comic anarchy in the writing of Gertrude Stein, Ezra Pound and others. Although I didn't necessarily want to write like them, to someone who's 20 years old that kind of work suggests freedom and possibility. It can make you see not only writing but the world itself in a completely different way."

Mr. DeLillo's new novel explores how Americans work and live abroad. The protagonist, James Axton, a "risk analyst" for a company with C.I.A. ties, becomes obsessed with a bizarre murderous cult whose members select their victims by their initials. Mr. DeLillo describes *The Names*, along with *Ratner's Star*, as a book that was especially difficult for him to write.

"The main character," he says, "resisted realization for a longer time than other characters have. It wasn't until I went away for five or six months without doing any work on the book that James Axton came alive for me. Before that, he seemed to resist entering the sentences I was writing. And every time I began to write about the cult I seemed to enter a period of anxiety. I'm not sure whether this was because I was having trouble bringing the cult members to life or whether I simply didn't want to face the reality of what they did. I wasn't sure I could be equal to the mysteriousness of the murders they committed.

"A writer can be perfectly happy with the character he creates who happens to be a mass murderer if the writer feels that his creation has been successful. But in this case, it simply didn't work that way. The characters themselves made me wish I'd decided to do a simpler novel."

Like *Ratner's Star*, a book in which Mr. DeLillo says he tried to "produce a piece of mathematics," *The Names* is complexly structured and layered. It concludes with an excerpt from a novel in progress by Axton's 9-year-old son, Tap. Inspiration for the ending came from Atticus Lish, the young son of Mr. DeLillo's friend Gordon Lish, an editor.

"At first," Mr. DeLillo says, "I had no intention of using excerpts from Tap's novel. But as the novel drew to a close I simply could not resist. It seemed to insist on being used. Rather than totally invent a piece of writing that a 9-year-old boy might do, I looked at some of the work that Atticus had done when he was 9. And I used it. I used half a dozen sentences from Atticus's work. More important, the simple exuberance of his work helped me to do the last pages of the novel. In other words, I stole from a kid."

Young Atticus is given ample credit in the book's acknowledgments, but creative borrowing from life is not a new technique for Mr. DeLillo, who has been praised for his ear for dialogue. "The interesting thing about trying to set down dialogue realistically," he says, "is that if you get it right it sounds stylized. Why is it so difficult to see clearly and to hear clearly? I don't know. But it is, and in *Players* I listened very carefully to people around me. People in buses. People in the street. And in many parts of the book I used sentences that I heard literally, word for word. Yet it didn't sound as realistic as one might expect. It sounded over-refined even."

For three years while writing *The Names* Mr. DeLillo lived in Greece and traveled through the Middle East and India. "What I found," he says, "was that all this traveling taught me how to see and hear all over again. Whatever ideas about language may be in *The Names*, I think the most important thing is what I felt in hearing people and watching them gesture—in listening to the sound of Greek and Arabic and Hindi and Urdu. The simple fact that I was confronting new landscapes and fresh languages made me feel almost duty bound to get it right. I would see and hear more clearly than I could in more familiar places."

Living abroad also gave Mr. DeLillo a fresh perspective on the United States. "The thing that's interesting about living in another country," he says, "is that it's difficult to forget you're an American. The actions of the American Government won't let you. They make you self-conscious, make you aware of yourself as an American. You find yourself mixed up in world politics in more subtle ways than you're accustomed to. On the one hand, you're aware of America's blundering in country after country. And on the other hand, you're aware of the way in which people in other countries have created the myth of America, of the way in which they use America to relieve their own fears and guilt by blaming America automatically for anything that goes wrong."

Critic Diane Johnson has written that Mr. DeLillo's books have gone unread because "they deal with deeply shocking things about America that people would rather not face."

"I do try to confront realities," Mr. DeLillo responds. "But people would rather read about their own marriages and separations and trips to Tanglewood. There's an entire school of American fiction which might be called around-the-house-and-in-the-yard. And I think people like to read this kind of work because it adds a certain luster, a certain significance to their own lives."

The writer to whom Mr. DeLillo has most often been likened and for whom he has great respect is Thomas Pynchon. "Somebody quoted Norman Mailer as saying that he wasn't a better writer because his contemporaries weren't better," he says. "I don't know whether he really said that or not, but the point I want to make is that no one in Pynchon's generation can make that statement. If we're not as good as we should be it's not because there isn't a standard. And I think Pynchon, more than any other writer, has set the standard. He's raised the stakes."

Mr. DeLillo also praises William Gaddis for extending the possibilities of the novel by taking huge risks and making great demands on his readers. Yet many readers complain about the abstruseness of much contemporary writing.

"A lot of characters," Mr. DeLillo says, "have become pure act. The whole point in certain kinds of modern writing is that characters simply do what they do. There isn't a great deal of thought or sentiment or literary history tied up in the actions of characters. Randomness is always hard to absorb."

Mr. DeLillo believes that it is vital that readers make the effort. "The best reader," he says, "is one who is most open to human possibility, to understanding the great range of plausibility in human actions. It's not true that modern life is too fantastic to be written about successfully. It's that the most successful work is so demanding." It is, he adds, as though our better writers "feel that the novel's vitality requires risks not only by them but by readers as well. Maybe it's not writers alone who keep the novel alive but a more serious kind of reader."

A Novelist Faces His Themes on New Ground

Mervyn Rothstein / 1987

From *The New York Times*, December 20, 1987, pp. 5, 19. © 1987 *The New York Times*. Reprinted with permission.

Six themes in search of an author:

Theme 1: Death

The main subject of Don DeLillo's 1985 American Book Award-winning novel, *White Noise*—with its toxic spill and its college chairman of the department of Hitler studies—was death, or more specifically, the fear of death. As one character says, "Tibetans try to see death for what it is. It is the end of attachment to things . . . Dying is an art in Tibet . . . Here we don't die, we shop. But the difference is less marked than you think."

Now after eight novels, the 51-year-old Mr. DeLillo has written his first play—*The Day Room* directed by Michael Blakemore and starring, among others, Mary Beth Hurt and Mason Adams. It opens today at the Manhattan Theater Club, and while it isn't about death, the awareness of death is certainly there—"We can't meet death on our own terms," says one character toward the end of the play. "We have no terms. Our speeches rattle in our throats. We're robbed of all consolations. We're fully aware and completely helpless. We're borderline from the day we're born. Our only hope is other people."

Act One of *The Day Room* takes place in a hospital, part of which is a psychiatric wing. Two patients are visited by another patient, some doctors and nurses. Or are they? Which part are we in? Are the doctors doctors? Are the nurses nurses? Are the patients patients?

Act Two, a play within the Act One play in which the nine actors take on different roles, is set in a seedy motel room.

Some critics have seen a connection with Pirandello. But what *The Day Room* is about, Mr. DeLillo says, "is performance and perception—it's about acting, in a peculiar way, not acting as a craft, but acting as a model of human identity."

"I think theater is really mysterious and alluring for someone who has written a novel." Mr. DeLillo says, "and it seemed natural to me beginning a play that theater itself would be one of the subjects I was interested in. And I began to sense a connection, almost a metaphysical connection, between the craft of acting and the fear we all have of dying. It seemed to me that actors are a kind of model for the ways in which we hide from the knowledge we inevitably possess of our final extinction. There's a sense in which actors teach us how to hide. There's something about the necessary shift in identity which actors make in the ordinary course of their work that seems almost a guide to concealing what we know about ourselves. I think this is at the heart of the Act Two speech in which one actress addresses not only the characters on stage but the audience in the theater and says, "We show you how to hide from what you know.' "

Theme 2: Theater

Mr. DeLillo turned to the theater, he says, because he "had an idea of a man in a hospital being threatened by his immediate circumstances."

"I knew at once," he says, "that this man was in a bed in a room on a stage, and there was never any question but that this was an idea for a play, and I simply sat down and started writing dialogue."

The stage is very different from the typewriter, he says. "For one thing, when you're finished with a play, you don't have an object you hold in your hand and say. 'This is what I've done.' You're not quite sure what you've done. Rehearsals vary, performances vary. The play will be in book form, but that's not really the play—this is the play. And yet it's very elusive to try to determine a definitive performance, even a definitive moment, because they change all the time.

"Another important difference," he says, "is working with other people. I go to rehearsals mainly to eat—they have nice snacks. But I also go to enter that particular, sealed-off world of the play. We rehearsed in an old longshoreman's hall. It was odd, but the minutes passed very slowly, and the days passed quickly—it was a little like a sea voyage, and I lost a sense of the customary reference points.

"When we did this play in Cambridge, at Robert Brustein's American Repertory Theater, I was taking a walk one morning and I heard someone call my name, and there was the director looking out a window. And within the course of the next two strides I saw a cast member crossing the street with her arms full of dry cleaning. There was no one else in sight. I had the feeling that the play had spilled out into the streets.

"For that one moment the world of the play had become the world itself—and this is like no other feeling I've had working on novels."

Theme 3: Culture

In her review of *White Noise* in the *New York Times Book Review*, Jayne Anne Phillips wrote that Mr. DeLillo in his work "dealt not so much with character as with culture, survival and the ever-increasing interdependence between the self and the national and world community."

"I think that's accurate," Mr. DeLillo says. "I certainly don't deal with character in this play, which makes it difficult for actors to do. And yet the play is very different from my novels.

"To a certain extent the play in its original inception was not at all analyzable, at least by me, and in the course of various reworkings of it I've begun to sense a structure. But it's not the kind of play one can easily discuss because it doesn't involve interrelationships between characters—it involves a sense of theater, and of acting, and of human identity.

"When I first conceived the play, the first act seemed to progress with the kind of curious logic of a dream—it seemed like all I had to do was sit down and transcribe the words from one level of consciousness to a more immediate one. Act Two was a different matter completely—in a way, Act Two is an attempt to explain the first half of the play to myself; in a way it's the play about the play.

Theme 4: Illusion vs. Reality

Critics who saw the play in Massachusetts talked about the idea of illusion and reality, and some, in addition to tracing Mr. DeLillo's influences to Pirandello, added a dash of Samuel Beckett.

"I didn't have illusion and reality in mind," he says. "I guess I'm interested in the way the play forms a kind of unending circular structure—it bends back on itself. This has greater significance to me than any sense of what is real and what isn't. To me, it's all real, but it's happening in different levels, sometimes simultaneously."

As far as the influences on him, he says, "I'm not a student of theater, and at least in the early stages of this play I was working very close to my instinct. That's really all I can say about it. I haven't studied Pirandello. I've enjoyed Beckett's work but I don't think that I've been influenced by him."

Theme 5: Hospitals and Motels

Act One of *The Day Room* takes place in a hospital.

"The hospital is a place we don't necessarily expect to walk out of once we've entered," Mr. DeLillo says, "and this makes a hospital rather unique. I would simply say that a hospital room is an extreme condition, and much of the writing I've done, I think, is set in extreme places or extreme states of mind. It's a kind of terminus in this case, a terminus perhaps with a false bottom—a bottom in which we sense another reality, the reality of Act Two."

Act Two's setting is a motel.

"A motel is a peculiar reality—not exactly the same reality as a hospital, but it does represent a peculiar form of nowhere, particularly motels in undefined parts of the landscape. You don't know quite where you are, and for a brief time-perhaps not quite who you are."

Theme 6: Television

In *White Noise*, one character describes television as "the primal force in the American home, sealed off, self-contained, self-referring." In *The Day Room*, one character is a television set, and it has much to say.

"I lived abroad for three years," Mr. DeLillo says, "and when I came back to this country in 1982, I began to notice something on television which I hadn't noticed before. This was the daily toxic spill—there was the news, the weather and the toxic spill. This was a phenomenon no one even mentioned. It was simply a television reality. It's only the people who were themselves involved in these terrible events who seemed to be affected by them. No one even talked about them. This was one of the motivating forces of *White Noise*."

Theme 1: Death

"It seemed to me further that in the three years I'd been away, a sense of death had begun to permeate not only television but the media in general. Death seems to be all around us—in the newspapers, in magazines, on television, on the radio. Much of this, of course, is welcome news—new scientific developments which help us live longer. Nevertheless, I can't imagine a culture more steeped in the idea of death. I can't imagine what it's like to grow up in America today.

I can't imagine what it's like to be a child, surrounded by the specter of death."

Six themes in search of an author:
"Who knows why a theme chose me," Mr. DeLillo says. "I really can't say. It's very hard to discuss why certain themes develop. This is why we write about people and places, because the themes are sort of out of reach. I've always sensed as I entered a book that things began to happen just outside the range of the immediate action. It's simply the way my mind works. There's very little sense of a logic behind it."

An Interview with Don DeLillo

Kevin Connolly / 1988

From *The Brick Reader*, Ed. Linda Spalding and Michael Ondaatje (Toronto: Coach House Press, 1991), pp. 260–269. Reprinted by permission of Kevin Connolly.

American Don DeLillo began writing professionally when he was in his mid-thirties, beginning with *Americana* (1971). Since then, he has published nine novels, including *Players, Great Jones Street, Running Dog, The Names,* and *White Noise,* which earned him the American Book Award for 1985. A writer of unusual range, DeLillo has tackled topics as diverse as rock 'n' roll, terrorism, pornography, international intelligence, and college football in styles which often blur traditional boundaries between genres—from psychological drama to political thriller, science fiction to satire. Much admired by his peers, DeLillo has a reputation for being largely indifferent to commercial success. Until recently, he has enjoyed a degree of privacy uncommon among writers of his stature. DeLillo's novel *Libra* promises to change all of that. The novel deals with a topic for which the public, after twenty-five years, still has an insatiable appetite: the November 1963 assassination of U.S. President John F. Kennedy. In creating *Libra*, he has invented characters to complement his fictionalized versions of the key figures, but in most significant respects the novel draws on detail which is consistent with the facts, as we know them. Given the sheer volume and inconsistency of these facts, that in itself is no mean feat.

DeLillo was interviewed by Kevin Connolly in Toronto in 1988.

Connolly: I wanted to ask you a little about research—the effect of research on what you've taken pains to point out is a novel.

DeLillo: Well, I did do extensive research, and the heart of it was the Warren Report and its twenty-six volumes of testimony and exhibits. The first fifteen volumes contain the testimony of hundreds of people, ranging from witnesses to the assassination to people who knew the main figures involved. It's like an encyclopaedia of daily life. You learn a great deal which has nothing to do with the case itself, ranging from interesting regional speech patterns to the particularities of occupations. What it was like to be a train man in

25

Fort Worth in 1963. Waitresses, stripteasers, private detectives, all sorts of people trot out their lives, their theories, and so forth. So it was not only an education in an immediate sense, it provided a nice background on the fifties and sixties in many ways.

Connolly: And gave you the type of detail you needed for the novel.
DeLillo: Not only the detail but also the voices of certain characters. The Marguerite Oswald in the novel is, in most important respects, the Marguerite Oswald of the Warren Commission report. She spoke to the commission lawyers for a number of days and for hundreds of pages. So I found out a great deal from this, not only about her life and about Lee's life, but about how she speaks, how she thinks, and so on. It's interesting that her conspiracy theories have been borne out, if not in fact, then in that so many serious commentators on the case ended up coming to the same conclusions she came to instinctively and maternally. I also travelled to New Orleans, Dallas, Fort Worth, and Miami. Seeing the places where Oswald lived was particularly haunting. They're old houses that are in much the same condition as they were twenty-five years ago, and they stand in a kind of haunted aura, full of mystery and regret. I felt a similar sensation in Dealey Plaza itself. It's the loneliest place in Dallas, even with all the traffic buzzing past it. From my hotel window I could see tourists standing on the lawns and gesturing up to the sixth-floor window of the Texas Schoolbook Depository and down towards the triple underpass, and it was eerie. Like a kind of local tai chi exercise.

Connolly: Did you find anything in your research that you found burdensome as a writer, details you felt you couldn't omit, things you wish didn't exist?
DeLillo: No. In fact I found the research invigorating. It was the factual detail that drove the novel forward, that provided a motor. In important ways all I really had to do was follow these lives onto the pages in my typewriter. Aside from the fact that I needed a great deal of factual information to drive the book, the simple reality that these lives were so interesting came up. Not only Oswald and his wife and his mother, and Jack Ruby; but many other peripheral characters as well. Characters some readers will assume are fictional are in fact straight from the pages of history.

Connolly: Was there anything particular that you ran into that you remember as being important in producing the novel *Libra* as opposed to any number of possible novels you could have written when you were starting out?
DeLillo: I think what made the novel what it finally became was not anything I learned from my research so much as themes which began to develop themselves as I continued to work, chapter to chapter. It seems to me, finally, that what this book is about is history and dreams. Dreams meaning all those forces in our lives that are outside history. Most importantly, coincidence, for example. There is coincidence in the story itself, but it didn't suggest itself as a major theme to me until I was well into the book. I think the character of Ferrie impels Oswald toward that moment in history, in trying to convince him that he ought to step outside history to find his self-fulfillment. In 1963, Oswald committed two acts of violence. He also took a shot at General Walker, a famous right-wing figure in Dallas, and this was an act informed by a strict political motivation. I think that by the time Oswald fired at President Kennedy he had begun to unravel. I think the assassination was a much more complex act, driven, in the novel in any case, by coincidence and by fantasy to a certain extent. In this respect, Oswald predates other would-be assassins like John Hinkley Jr., who took a shot at President Reagan, and Arthur Bremer, who tried to kill Governor Wallace. Young men acting out of a backdrop of fantasy and disaffection.

Connolly: One of the characters in the novel comments on these kinds of people, saying that they no longer have to live "lives of quiet desperation . . ."
DeLillo: Yes. Suddenly it is possible to shape your desperation, to find a destiny for it. It didn't have to be quiet. You suddenly *could* enter history, as long as you were willing to spend it in prison.

Connolly: The character of Nicholas Branch interested me from an authorial point of view, not just because he is also a writer, but because he almost seems to be a nightmare image of you, had you tried to write something that was historically accurate.
DeLillo: He had a tougher time than I did. Of course he was writing history and I was writing fiction. But what I was trying to express with Branch was, I guess, two main things. One was the enormous amount of material that the assassination generated, material which eventually makes Branch almost impotent. He simply cannot keep up with it: the path changes as he writes.

The material itself becomes, after a while, the subject. The other thing I wanted to do with Branch was to suggest the ways the American conscious- ness has changed since the assassination. I think that what has been mis- sing for the past twenty-five years is a sense of the coherent reality most Americans share. It's almost as if we enter the world of randomness and ambiguity. Branch himself refers to this as an "aberration in the heartland of the real." Even after all these years we still can't agree on the number of gun- men, the number of shots, the time span between the shots, the number of wounds on the President's body, the size and shape of those wounds. And even beyond this confusion of data there's a sense of the secret manipulation of history. This has certainly entered our mass consciousness. Documents are lost or concealed. Official records are sealed for fifty or seventy-five years. A curious number of suspicious murders and suicides. And I think this current runs from November of 1963 right through Viet Nam and Watergate, and into Iran-Contra.

Connolly: It's almost as if these hearings have become societal rites of pas- sage. They seem to pop up every ten or fifteen years.
DeLillo: Exactly. But it's something we have to go through almost as a token of memory, as a memorialization of the first time it happened.

Connolly: I was wondering if you had been watching the Iran-Contra hear- ings while you were writing *Libra?*
DeLillo: No.

Connolly: Because the first things I thought about when I ran into the peo- ple in your book were the impressions I had while watching those hearings. What struck me first was how mundane and toothless these people seemed to be—people like Secord and North and Poindexter. They came across as com- pletely unremarkable people. The other thing I noticed was how compelled I was to watch something which was essentially boring, in its presentation, and everything else. It became almost an unconscious pursuit of secrecy.
DeLillo: Someone said to me that to find the roots of the Iran-Contra all you had to do was look at *Running Dog.* A CIA proprietary becomes a way to gen- erate vast personal profits. A fake company set up as a conduit for espionage becomes a vast profit-making apparatus on its own, which may have been what happened in Iran-Contra. Many people think it obviously did.

Connolly: Terrorism and intelligence become business.
DeLillo: Yes, exactly.

Connolly: A lot of people would think that that kind of thing must have
something to do with ideology.
DeLillo: I don't think it's nearly so much about ideology as it is about suc-
ceeding in the world. Personal power and profit.

Connolly: One of the things I've noticed in your work, and in particular the
novels which touch on covert action, is the presence of faith as an issue. In
the new novel it's a little bit different from novels like *Players* and *Running
Dog*, I think. And I understand that your background is in theology and philosophy. Selvy, for example, in *Running Dog*, is described by one of the other
characters as a "believer," someone who would do clandestine work for nothing. But when you are confronted with Selvy's character, he seems to be indifferent to ideology. His faith expresses itself more in things like how to fire a
handgun properly.
DeLillo: Exactly. His faith is in tradecraft. But in the world of *Running Dog* I
think the only true believers are the Mafia. Because they're a family in the
general and the specific sense of the word. This is what binds them, a sense of
blood relationships and a very long tradition of doing what they are doing.
But there's a surge of acquisitiveness in *Running Dog* which peters out as
soon as all of the players get their hands on the object. They seem immediately to lose interest. I think this was a feeling I had about the country in
those particular years, in the late seventies. It was interesting that some years
after, after the Hitler diaries surfaced, there was the same kind of acquisitiveness going on, but on a much larger scale. In a way I was naive about what
might happen if this Hitler film [in *Running Dog*] suddenly surfaced. When
the diaries surfaced there was a much greater reaction. Entire publishing
empires went totally berserk over these fake diaries. And it died out immediately afterwards.

Connolly: I can see a similarity between Selvy and some of the characters
you have created in *Libra*. Why the interest in people whose lives are so
focussed on secrecy, people who in many ways are completely divorced from
any real sense of community?
DeLillo: Most of my novels seem to turn on a character who ends up alone
in a small room. I don't know why that is exactly. And it's curious that in

moving towards the assassination I finally came up against a *real* character who spent a significant amount of time in a small room alone. Of course that was Oswald himself, who planned the murder of General Walker in a room only slightly larger than a closet, who spent time in the brig [in the Marines], who lived in a rooming house in Dallas in a room about the size of a jail cell, and who finally ended up in a real jail cell, before he himself was killed.

In *Libra* I tried to trace secrecy back to childhood through Win Everett's daughter, Suzanne. Win thinks about secrecy in terms of a child's secrets and how important they are to her. He thinks it's dangerous to give up your secrets because in doing so you lose some of your identity, some of your grip on the world. It seemed to me that secrets—the pleasure and the conflict of secrets—remained the same through your entire life. I think it was Octavio Paz who said that man spies on himself, and eventually I think this is what happens to Win Everett in *Libra*. He begins to examine himself as a subject, as someone in the third person.

Connolly: At the end of *Libra* you've included an author's note, but despite what you say there, and what you've said to various people in articles about *Libra* being a novel, and how it should be treated as such, you still have people writing letters to the *New York Times* complaining about your accuracy on certain counts.

DeLillo: I've answered that letter, which is just a misinterpretation of what happens in the novel. The fellow who wrote the letter was assistant counsel to the Warren Commission, and his feeling is that Jack Ruby's murder of Oswald could not possibly have been carefully planned, for reasons he details in the letter. And in fact, in the novel, it is not carefully planned at all.

Connolly: It's a coincidence.
DeLillo: Yes, it's more or less a coincidence. Ruby, obscurely motivated as always, was more or less on his way to send twenty-five dollars to one of his stripteasers and/or to shoot Oswald.

Connolly: Are you surprised about the direction in which this issue of accuracy has gone since the novel was published? I guess what I want is for you to expand on that tantalizing remark you make at the end of the author's note to the effect that fiction can be a kind of refuge from the uncertainties of fact.
DeLillo: I'm not so sure now that was such a good idea. The afterword is really a dressed-up legal disclaimer. Possibly I shouldn't have dressed it up.

But I didn't want one or two stark sentences disclaiming any resemblance between characters in the book and certain living characters. In a theoretical sense I think fiction can be a refuge and a consolation. In *Libra* the national leader still dies, but for one thing, at least we know how it happens. Beyond that, fiction offers patterns and symmetry that we don't find in the experience of ordinary living. Stories are consoling, fiction is one of the consolation prizes for having lived in the world.

Connolly: It seems as though you've anticipated the fact that with a thing as naturally paranoia-producing as the Kennedy assassination, people are going to come up with their own answers for what might have happened. It could be as simple as saying, "Oh, Hoover had him killed, it's obvious." It seems in the afterword you've anticipated treading on other peoples' fictions.
DeLillo: I suppose I was saying to people who've read lightly in the non-fiction end of the spectrum that it's possible to imagine the assassination having happened in this way and therefore to move to the edge of the spectrum other obsessions and other possibilities. Doing this helps us to understand not just the characters in the novel but character itself and human motivation, and the forces of chance and coincidence on the way characters act.

Connolly: Something that would be lost if you were simply faced with all of that information.
DeLillo: I think so. None of the material I've read has ever attempted to enter the minds of Oswald or Ruby, and none of it treats them as flawed humans. They're always treated as people who would automatically move from spot A to spot B in the straightest possible line. And the reality is that these were the last two men in the world who would ever behave in that way. This is in fact what is behind Ruby's shooting of Oswald. All the junk and torn newspapers in Ruby's consciousness are not only part of what he was, but probably the major part.

Connolly: I wanted to ask you a little more about history. In recent years there has been a spate of films, books, short stories, and so on, trying to deal with recent history. Viet Nam is the most obvious example. And it seems to me the way you've approached recent history is different from the way most other artists appear to be approaching it. There seems to be a kind of moralistic digestion of the Viet Nam experience, an interpretation of what it means on extremely simplified levels.

DeLillo: You're thinking of *Platoon*.

Connolly: Among others. One of the blurbs on the back of the paperback edition of *Running Dog* praises it as one of the best novels about Viet Nam. It had never occurred to me that *Running Dog* was about Viet Nam in anything but a peripheral way. Given all of this appetite for commentary on recent history, I was wondering if you think about your own responsibility as a fictional interpreter when you are dealing with material which is so current?

DeLillo: Yes. First, in writing *Libra* I did feel a strong sense of responsibility. Much more I think, than most novelists feel while writing a particular novel. But I never forgot that I was doing a novel and not a piece of history. In a way *Libra* is about history. But it certainly is not history itself. I tell people, when they want to know what to call this book, that it's a novel. I don't think of it as a non-fiction novel or a "novel-as-history," or any of those designations which have been used in the past. Or even as a historical novel, which technically I suppose it is.

To me the history seems too recent for that. It's about history in a way. It's also about fiction, about plot-making, and the relationships between plots and deaths, something which I first encountered while I was writing *White Noise*, and which I've developed somewhat in *Libra*. Mainly through the character of Win Everett, who thinks that the more tightly one plots a story, the more likely it is to end in death. Detective novels most often have a corpse turn up at some point. And so the plot Win devises in the larger world will turn out the same way. Even though he does not want a death at the end of it, it will naturally happen that way because this is the nature of plots; they move inevitably towards death, both in the world of books, and the world outside books.

Connolly: The novels I've read of yours have a much greater emphasis on plot or storyline than a lot of literary fiction these days. They are also psychological studies, but I think plot is always prominent. Do you prefer to work with plot; do you like to keep the reader hooked that way?

DeLillo: I think the reason is partly the novels you've mentioned. They are all more carefully plotted than my other novels, simply because they are about conspiracy, or about terrorist plots, as in the case of *Players*. When I started

writing *Players* my only plan was to write a novel about the way people naturally talk to each other, all the time, and in particular people who are intimate with each other—as it turned out, Pammy and Lyle. The whole novel
was simply going to be dialogue hetween two fairly typical New Yorkers of a
certain age. Certainly Pammy is, Lyle is a little stranger, not really typical of
anything. But very early on, I abandoned this. I found a murder taking place
on the floor of the Stock Exchange and I followed that path. This automatically supplied me with a sense of plot I had no intention of producing earlier.

Connolly: It took me a while to get used to the way your characters speak; I
think it might take a lot of people who are used to traditional literary dialogue a while to get a sense of where you're coming from. Your dialogue is
clipped and idiosyncratic to fit the way people actually speak. You explained
where it came from in the new novel, from the Warren transcripts, but from
reading some of your other work it's obviously not a new thing. Is duplicat-
ing actual speech something you are interested in?

DeLillo: The only time I consciously tried to do it was in *Players*, again
because the novel started as endless dialogue between a husband and wife. I
wanted to get it the way people actually spoke it. It is my theory that if you
record dialogue as people actually speak it, it will seem stylized to the reader.
It will seem like a conscious attempt to shape dialogue when in fact it's *literally* the way people speak to each other. I listened to people very carefully
around the period I was writing *Players*, and the result is what you see on the
page. Of course it's the dialogue of certain people; it's not the way everyone
speaks. But there's a certain strata of New York society in which people speak
the way they do in *Players*. As far as I'm concerned it's word for word, literally
like that. In *Libra* I had the benefit of printed dialogue in which people were
talking, I think fairly comfortably, to Commission lawyers. And I got much of
that, particularly Marguerite Oswald, right out of the Warren Report.

Connolly: Some people would argue that you can't do that and expect to get
literate dialogue. I think it's a bit of a shock to people what it actually looks
like transcribed. You do what playwrights often do, taking advantage of the
verbal accidents that clipping sentences and colloquialism create.

DeLillo: Right. This is something you could study for the rest of your life and
attempt to write properly for the rest of your life. And you'd probably never
do it the same way from book to book, because real dialogue, as spoken, is

always a little different as you move one millimetre from one social strata to another. It changes so much that you could develop a whole new theory of it just by listening to it.

Connolly: Are you especially conscious of what your writing is doing as you're writing it? Do you usually structure your novels in advance?
DeLillo: No. Not at all.

Connolly: It's more organic than that?
DeLillo: Yes, absolutely. Again, *Libra* is an exception because the life of Oswald and the other characters suggested a kind of sequence that I'd have to follow.

Connolly: You have an obvious point to which everything moves.
DeLillo: The two streams actually converge. The Oswald chapters and the conspiracy chapters actually converge at the end of the long New Orleans chapter when Ferrie talks to Oswald. He in fact explains the plot of the book in explaining that what they in fact want from him is for him to assassinate the president. He is actually laying out the plot for the novel *Libra* there because they turn out to be the same thing, these two streams converging: one, Oswald's life; two, this plot against the president's life.

Throughout the novel, Oswald's viewpoint is predominant in the Oswald chapters. In the conspiracy chapters, Oswald is only talked about or distantly glimpsed. Once the two streams merge there is no longer this chapter-by-chapter sense of a separation of viewpoints. Oswald appears in what were essentially their chapters. His viewpoint is suddenly introduced into other people's chapters, and vice versa. The book becomes one headlong scream towards November 22.

Connolly: The scene immediately following the assassination, after the shots were fired. How much of that is imagination, and how much of it is what you actually know? It's a part of the novel I admire a great deal. It's got the literary equivalent of a handheld camera feel to it.
DeLillo: That's a good description of it. It all happened, I mean I actually walked the route he most likely travelled in the neighbourhood of his rooming house in the Oak Cliff section of Dallas. Nobody knows why Oswald shot patrolman Tippet. Anti-Warren people think that Oswald in fact did not

shoot Tippet, that somebody else shot him, or that there were two people shooting. But I'm convinced that Oswald killed him; the gun was found on him when he was captured. It's all true as far as Oswald is concerned. What happened in the theatre is also true except for the presence of Wayne Elko, a fictional character, in the back row.

Connolly: The symbol of the woman's shoes left on the hood of patrolman Tippet's car . . .
DeLillo: This happened.

Connolly: It struck me as extremely important as you set it up in the novel. Where your novel is satisfying as an explanation, albeit a fictional one, of the assassination is that it acknowledges the almost mystical presence of coincidence. And the woman's shoes seem to incorporate that mystery. Because there turns out to be a perfectly natural human reason for them being there, but at the time they're found it's almost spooky.
DeLillo: Think of the cops standing around the car wondering where this pair of shoes came from. [The woman who found Tippet was a nurse and she left her extra pair of work shoes there in the confusion.] It's totally bizarre. But it did happen. When this is first introduced at the beginning of the novel in a scene with Nicholas Branch he thinks of it as a "holy moment." You used the word mystical. And that's what it is to me too. It's a kind of accidental holiness, a randomness so intense and surrounded by such violence that it takes on nearly a sacred inexplicability. And as you noted it's so strangely real at the same time. That's what I was aiming at.

Connolly: The structure of some of your other works interested me as well. *Libra* is traditional in the sense that you build towards a climax and then there's a dropping off near the end. But most of your novels seem to use nontraditional structures. *Players*, for example, seems to dissolve rather than build to a climax. Plots are initiated, and then seem to untie themselves towards the end. There's a scene at the end of *Players* in which Lyle lies on the bed in front of a motel window. The light's pouring in and you get a vision of him breaking into pieces in the light.
DeLillo: The novel is also breaking apart in order to regenerate itself. At the beginning of the novel we hear a discussion about motels, which is where the novel ends. I think there's also a blinding flash of light which anticipates

the one at the end of the novel. That seems to happen in my books, and I wasn't really aware of it until somebody pointed it out. There's a looping action from the end of the book to the beginning.

Connolly: That feeling of things breaking up, everything moving towards entropy, seems to connect with some of the ideas in *Libra*. All of that information which swallows Branch becomes so rationally overwhelming. Is this something you believe in general, about life or American society?
DeLillo: No. I don't know why certain currents run through my books. They're not necessarily based on logical convictions I have about the world outside the novel. Some of them are almost abstract patterns, like the way painters repeat lines or colours. I repeat them, and I'm not always conscious that I'm doing it.

Connolly: You're not compelled to pull it apart rationally?
DeLillo: No . . .

Connolly: Is that a superstition you have, or is it just something that doesn't interest you?
DeLillo: It's not a superstition. But I don't try to do it because I don't think I know how. I wouldn't be able to do it if I tried. And if I thought I could, I probably wouldn't do it anyway. So maybe it is a superstition. [*laughs*]

Connolly: The other pattern I wanted to ask you about, and I guess this is also specific to your novels about intelligence agencies, is the tendency of things, once they become extremely sophisticated, to turn the motivations of their users or creators towards the primitive. The whole set-up of the PAC/ORD company in *Running Dog* seems to reflect that tendency. For example, Selvy's self-worth is based on very primitive impulses. He's like an animal in some ways.
DeLillo: People are sometimes reduced to their essentials in my fiction. *White Noise*, if I had to summarize it briefly, studies the idea that the more advanced technology becomes, the more primitive our fear becomes. In *Ratner's Star* there is a much more elaborate discussion of the connection between modern minds and the primitive, mysticism and science, and how one curiously begins to shade into the other. I think one of the effects of

solitude is that you are eventually reduced to a more essential being, and this does happen to Selvy in *Running Dog.*

Connolly: Characters in your books also tend to emphasize the importance of naming things. Lyle experiences it, and certainly Oswald does. Oswald is constantly writing in his diary and trying to actualize things he dreams about by using the words. Lyle does it in *Players*, he focusses intensely on names and numbers, as if he were getting a kind of primitive understanding from that.

DeLillo: I think naming things helps us hold the world together, almost literally. Without naming I think it would all fall apart. Names are the sub-atomic glue of the human world, and for a certain type of mentality, the clandestine mentality like Lyle's or like Oswald's, naming becomes a secret act, secret and obsessive. I think people do it as a way of keeping their grip on the world, and I think Oswald's dyslexia made it a problem for him to see the world as a coherent set of facts and words and ideas.

Connolly: It's interesting that something which he has so much trouble with becomes so important to master and control. Even when he doesn't understand the Marx he is reading he's absolutely convinced of its importance.

DeLillo: Yes, and he didn't know that he was dyslexic. Nobody knew, apparently. It wasn't until after he died, after the psychologists studied his writing that they could tell he had this problem. He felt that he knew things, yet they continued to elude him. He just couldn't get a grip on them.

Connolly: Critics I have read who are equivocal about your writing—there was a review of *Libra* in a recent issue of *Mother Jones* that was like this— tend to admire the craft and the technique while complaining about what they see as a lack of depth in your characters. Other people take the approach that the writing is paranoid. In a recent article in the *New York Review of Books*, Robert Towers called you the "chief shaman of the paranoid school of American fiction." And I was wondering what your reaction is to this kind of criticism.

DeLillo: It didn't annoy me. I could take it as an observation about *Libra* and not disagree strongly. I don't consider myself paranoid at all. I think I see things exactly as they are. William Burroughs has said that the paranoid is the man in possession of the facts. Once you know the facts, people who don't think you're crazy. It's impossible to write about the Kennedy assassination and its aftermath without taking note of twenty-five years of paranoia which has collected around that event. This is one of the major functions of Nicholas Branch in the novel, of Marguerite Oswald as well. Simply to give the reader an idea of the psychic energies which have flowed from November 1963. One of the major energies is paranoia. But you don't have to be paranoid to write about this, or to understand it.

So that's my answer to that statement, which was probably meant as a compliment. He did mention me with Pynchon and Mailer, and that's pretty good company.

Connolly: I'm wondering if you've thought about the relationship between your writing and your politics. Because there are certain things you write about that other people might consider paranoid for political reasons.
DeLillo: I certainly don't try consciously to make political statements or to include political material. It depends on how you define politics, I suppose. In a way everything we do is politics. Very few critics have commented on *Libra* in those terms. The one who did, though, was very adamant about it; I was virtually an agent of Moammar Ghaddafi. [*laughs*] I don't know how to respond to that, because it's certainly not surprising that you learn something about a novelist by reading his fiction, without hearing any of his public utterances. Of course you do; what I write is what I am. Aside from the fact that it must naturally flow into one's books, I certainly don't have any political program. Not only for my books, but for my life or for the life of my country.

Connolly: I guess if you grapple with a topic you are interested in, people are always going to fall on one side or another of you.
DeLillo: Especially if it's a famous and tragic event as the assassination was. People will object to the fact that in the novel the CIA, at least renegade agents from the CIA, are to some extent behind it all. But it's hardly a leftist position to think that.

Connolly: The effect of film on your writing: I noticed it in the film that begins *Players*, the film which is the object of the pursuit in *Running Dog*. Most notable for me was the realization I came to while reading the assassination scene in *Libra*, about how my perception of that event was so completely determined by film, the amateur footage that was shot of the assassination, and so on. And I think you consciously worked that perception into the pacing of that scene.

DeLillo: Yes. Sure.

Connolly: Do you look at film technique and try to find an equivalent technique in your writing?

DeLillo: I've never thought about applying it to writing, but I was a very avid filmgoer through the sixties. That was my personal golden age of movies: Bergman, Antonioni, Godard, and several other people. I haven't been nearly so enthusiastic since those days. But I never thought of a novelistic counterpart to certain types of filmmaking. If this has seeped into my work, that's fine, but I've never taken a conscious crack at it.

Connolly: Have you had film producers interested in your work?

DeLillo: Now and then, yes. Usually someone in a borrowed office phones up and says, "You know, *Great Jones Street*, boy that's somethin'. Wow, let's have lunch." [*laughs*] Things like that. People have taken options and written screenplays, but I've never wanted to write screenplays for my own books. There is serious interest in *Libra*, but I don't know what's going to happen there. One of these days someone is going to ask me if I want to write a screenplay for *Libra*. I guess I'll decide then.

Seven Seconds

Ann Arensberg / 1988

From *Vogue*, August 1988, pp. 336–339, 390. Reprinted by permission of
Ann Arensberg.

Don DeLillo is a writer who addresses our feeling that something is out of
control, that we no longer share a coherent view of reality. DeLillo dates the
change in consciousness from the early 'sixties, from November 1963, to be
specific: November 22, Dealey Plaza, Dallas, Texas.

Don DeLillo published his first novel eight years later, in 1971. Critics, fellow novelists, and students of modern literature immediately identified him as
a candidate for lasting greatness, but it wasn't until he received the Award in
Literature from the American Academy and Institute of Arts and Letters in
1984, and the American Book Award the next year for his eighth book, *White
Noise*, that his extraordinary talents were more widely acknowledged. This
month, Viking will publish DeLillo's ninth novel, *Libra*, a fictional biography of
Lee Harvey Oswald. Coinciding with the twenty-fifth anniversary of the John
Kennedy assassination, it will finally introduce DeLillo to a larger audience.

What characterizes much of DeLillo's work is its location "in extreme
places or extreme states of mind." In *White Noise*, the Gladney family is
engulfed by a toxic chemical cloud released by an industrial accident. (Don
DeLillo has also been credited with prescience: the publication of *White
Noise* coincided with the chemical disaster at Bhopal.) And the protagonists
of *Great Jones Street, Players, Running Dog, The Names*, and, of course, *Libra*
all become entangled in conspiracies that they, half-consciously, have had a
hand in creating.

The extremest place of all, the seedbed of every conspiracy, is DeLillo's
America, a fantastic and yet all-too-recognizable culture of "rot and glut and
blare" dominated by an invasive technology that promises to prolong life
while threatening to extinguish the world. DeLillo's characters are death-
haunted urban creatures, living in a society from which Nature and feeling
have been excluded, feeding on a diet of abstractions or, in other words,
"plots." It is a universe in which Thoreauvian retreat is impossible, since
every character shares all the guilt and all the responsibility. As DeLillo writes

in *Libra*, "Everyone was a spook or dupe or asset, a double, courier, cutout or defector, or was related to one. We were all linked in a vast and rhythmic coincidence, a daisy chain of rumor, suspicion or secret wish."

In earlier novels, Victorian novels in particular, the individual battled to find a place in society. For DeLillo's people, notably for Oswald, sanity and integrity appear to depend on each one's remaining outside the mainstream of a society that is clearly dangerous, even fatal, to the individual. When DeLillo's Oswald acts alone, he has goals and ideals, however doomed; when he is beckoned and seduced by the many-headed forces of conspiracy, he loses any sense of self in the collective madness.

Writing about complexity may be DeLillo's ablest defense against his uncomfortable awareness of the anxieties, dreams, rhythms, and interconnections of modern life. But a front-line observer like DeLillo must devise his own methods of protection. In an era when too many writers are willing media-fodder, he lives quietly and privately, husbanding his energy to meet the demands of his work. A serious, handsome man, now fifty-one, he is as eloquent in person as he is on paper. The process of publication does not interfere with his daily routine: "I've always tried to maintain a certain detachment. I put everything into the book, and very little into what happens after I've finished it."

Ann Arensberg: Where were you on November 22, 1963?
Don DeLillo: Eating lunch on New York's West Side with a couple of friends. In a seafood restaurant called Davy Jones. I don't have a clear memory of the rest of that day; I guess I watched a little television. On Sunday, late Sunday, I did watch the Ruby shooting of Oswald for a couple of hours; but I didn't watch much of the funeral, which was Monday. I think I have a kind of habitual aversion to ceremony; that's all.

AA: Do you remember your feelings?
DDL: It was a great shock, the kind that resonates through the years. Somebody reminded me recently that the last paragraph of my first novel, *Americana*, is set in Dealey Plaza. The hero drives along the motorcade route with his hand on the horn, and that's how the novel ends. I had totally forgotten this.

AA: Do you think the Kennedy assassination is more real to us because it was photographed and televised? Or less real?

DDL: I think the Zapruder film makes it more real: the moment of death has a bluntness that is unforgettable. But, at the same time, it's all surrounded by blurs, shadows, and ambiguities. What happens to the President's head is a major reality of that particular day. But it's not a reality that lends itself to an understanding of the facts, beyond that this is the shot that kills him.

AA: You say in *Libra* that the JFK assassination was "the seven seconds that broke the back of the American century."
DDL: Perhaps it's a matter of other parts of the world beginning to catch up with us, but the assassination seemed to slow down our growth as the dominant world power. And it had an effect on Americans that we'll probably never recover from. The fact that it could happen. The fact that it was on film. The fact that two days later the assassin himself was killed on live television. All of these were psychological shock waves that are still rolling. The subsequent assassinations and attempted assassinations all seem part of the events of November 22nd.

AA: But isn't it possible that JFK himself broke the back of the American century? By portraying King Arthur and at the same time conspiring to kill Castro?
DDL: No, Kennedy's errors were not fully understood until long after he was dead. While he was alive, he was surrounded by positive forces and vibrations. A spirit of intelligence, grit, and vigor. The country was riding a benevolent whirlwind while he was in office. Most people still think of Kennedy mainly in positive ways.

AA: What made you realize that the Kennedy assassination was a topic you had to write about?
DDL: When I was working on *White Noise*, I interrupted it to do a nonfiction piece for *Rolling Stone* ["American Blood: A Journey Through the Labyrinth of Dallas and JFK"]. I never interupt my work, so there must have been a strong impulse, an impulse brought on by the uncertainty of the assassination itself, and by the mystery of Oswald's life.

AA: What was it that led you to construct your novel around him?
DDL: Personal incentive: I'd known that Oswald had spent time in the Bronx when he was a kid. When I learned that he had spent a year living only six or seven blocks from where I lived, I became more interested. And I learned that he played hookey at the Bronx Zoo, where I spent a fair amount of time. He

would have been thirteen; I would have been sixteen. Naturally, I wondered if I had ever run into him; that proximity gave me the final incentive. But it wasn't for three or four months, when I finally came upon a certain rhythm in my sentences, a kind of broken, abrupt rhythm that I equate with Oswald's inner life, that I felt I had found his voice and his spirit.

AA: You've written that Lee Harvey Oswald seems like a fictional character scripted out of doctored photos, tourist cards, mail-order forms, visa applications, altered signatures, and pseudonyms. How did you manage to negotiate that maze of aliases and uncover the real Oswald?

DDL: The real Oswald was naïve, self-pitying, paranoid, and occasionally violent. Certainly, he beat his wife. At the same time he was continually battered, and he had an enormous difficulty making his way in the world. It seemed natural to me that such a person would find a release, almost a child-like excitement, in other identities, in aliases.

AA: How would you describe your fictional Oswald?

DDL: The book is about the outsider who wants to belong. And it's also the story of a man who could go either way. Libra: the scale. Which way will the scale tip? Will Oswald go toward the left or toward the right? In direct reference to the assassination, he was a man of the left who ended up carrying out the wishes of the right wing.

AA: How was Oswald, as you portray him, different from would-be assassins like Bremer or Hinckley?

DDL: Oswald was, at least by his own lights, a pragmatic political man, even an idealist. He defected to Russia, a completely startling thing for someone of his background to do. Oswald's attempt on General Walker [the right-wing fanatic] was a purely political act. But, as I interpret it, his attempt on Kennedy was based on fantasy. He stepped outside history and let the forces of destiny move him where they would—nonhistorical forces like dreams, coincidences, intuitions, the alignment of the heavenly bodies, all these things. So he is a forerunner of John Hinckley and Arthur Bremer, both of whom walked two feet above the ground and evolved their own realities.

AA: You make a point of Oswald's dedication to words, and his terrible difficulty with them—his dyslexia and his struggle with reading, writing, and spelling.

DDL: I like to think of him, to a certain extent, as a frustrated writer. Certainly, he was an enthusiastic diarist for one period of his life. Before his defection, when he filled out an application for the Albert Schweitzer College in Switzerland, he said, "I want to write short stories about contemporary American life." Later, he wrote to Governor Connally from Russia in order to have his undesirable discharge overturned and said, "I am living here in much the same way E. Hemingway resided in Paris." These simple, bald statements were very interesting to me.

AA: The remarkable thing about *Libra* is that we identify with the assassins and the conspirators, whatever their morals, motives, or politics. How do you get your readers to set aside their preconceptions and ideologies?
DDL: I try to find one characteristic that points us toward the person's humanity; we are all equally human. I try not to supply sympathies and compassions, which I think either flow directly from the character to the reader or not. Also, a lot of the characters in this book, probably more than in my other books, are like people from my own neighborhood; the people who surround Jack Ruby, for example, and the organized crime figures. So it was easier, I think, than creating bankers in *The Names*.

AA: You have invented a fascinating character, Nicholas Branch, a retired CIA officer who is writing a secret history of the assassination for the Agency. You depict him as being inundated by documents and exhibits, until paper begins to slide out of the room and across the doorway. Did you feel overwhelmed by the volume of material you had to cover? What did your own study look like when you were working on *Libra*?
DDL: Not nearly so cluttered as his working quarters. The twenty-six volumes appended to the "Warren Commission Report" were the heart of the research I did. Fifteen volumes of testimony and eleven volumes of exhibits, from FBI reports to photographs of knotted string. Everything you could imagine—including descriptions of people firing weapons at goats' heads. I also read a lot of biographies and reports in places like the *Journal of Forensic Sciences*. But I found the research invigorating. I depended on it. I needed it. It continually helped me propel the story. Since the material deals mainly with people and their association with such a significant event, I didn't find it stale or dreary or difficult at all. And, of course, I still read in the case.

AA: How do you account for the tremendous proliferation of theories about the Kennedy assassination?

DDL: Simply by the ambiguity that surrounds the evidence. We are still trying to figure out how many shots were fired, how many times the President was hit, what the timespan was between shots, where exactly the wounds appear. There is confusion over the autopsy, over the autopsy reports—which were eventually burned. There is confusion over the fact that the President's brain disappeared from the National Archives. There are dozens of such anomalies.

AA: Do you feel that the "Warren Commission Report" was an attempt to cover up discrepancies in the evidence, to put a stop to speculation?

DDL: To my knowledge, there was no specific cover-up. It was an attempt to produce a report for the 1964 elections, so that some of the uncertainty would disappear and Johnson would not feel that it was trailing him and his potential voters into the ballot booths. But there are areas that should have been investigated that were immediately closed off, such as a very interesting incident involving Silvia Odio, the daughter of a celebrated anti-Castro leader, who claimed that Oswald and two Cubans appeared on her doorstep in Dallas on or about September 25th and said that we (meaning anti-Castro people) ought to assassinate President Kennedy. She was interviewed by lawyers for the Warren Commission, but no one followed up on her claim that Oswald and two anti-Castro Cubans had discussed killing the President.

AA: Have you chosen a subject for your next book?

DDL: No. But I think the topic of terrorism and art—"art" meaning "writing"—is an interesting one. I wonder if modern writers have felt preempted by terrorism, have felt that they've lost a certain influence that violence, a particular kind of theatrical violence, has seized from them. Mailer once said that he had hoped to alter the consciousness of our time. I wonder if any writer harbors such a thought now, in the light of what political terrorists have managed to do in that regard, and in so few years.

AA: What role can the writer play in our society at this late date in the century?

DDL: The writer is the person who stands outside society, independent of affiliation and independent of influence. The writer is the man or woman who automatically takes a stance against his or her government. There are so many temptations for American writers to become part of the system and part of the structure that now, more than ever, we have to resist. American writers ought to stand and live in the margins, and be more dangerous. Writers in repressive societies are considered dangerous. That's why so many of them are in jail.

AA: Do you feel a sense of kinship with your contemporaries?
DDL: O.K. Here's a speech for you. Think of the postwar generation of writers. I'm talking specifically about male writers. Styron, Mailer, Vidal, Baldwin, and so on. Then think of the subsequent generation. Pynchon. McElroy. McGuane. Stone. Myself. A couple of others. If you were to give each group a choice of writing a novel about John F. Kennedy or Lee Harvey Oswald, what would be the result? It seems to me that the first group would choose Kennedy, and the second group, my group, would almost invariably choose Oswald. ▽

PW Interviews: Don DeLillo

William Goldstein / 1988

From *Publishers Weekly*, August 19, 1988, pp. 55–6. Reprinted by permission.

The first question is, of course, where was he on November 22, 1963? "I was in a restaurant on the West Side of Manhattan having lunch with a couple of friends," says Don DeLillo, whose ninth novel, *Libra*, just published by Viking (Fiction Forecasts, July 1), is about Lee Harvey Oswald and the Kennedy assassination. "I heard just after lunch, in a bank, that the president had been shot in Dallas. I heard a bank teller tell another customer, and that was the beginning of it. I think that event had been in the back of my mind for a long time, and of course it's moved to the front of my mind since then."

DeLillo says he is "a little less reluctant" to talk about this book than he has been about his eight previous novels, which include the American Book Award—winning *White Noise*, because *Libra* "is grounded in history and because most of the key characters are real people and they come to us with an actual history, which isn't true of the invented characters in my other novels. My characters tend not to have histories, they exist within the margins of the page. It makes for difficult conversation about a book. All you can really do is point back to the writing itself or to the character himself. In this case, however, people like Oswald, Ruby, Marina and Marguerite Oswald and other characters provide a little more solid fare for conversation. And of course the other thing," DeLillo adds, "is that it was such a tragic and crucial event, and I feel a certain responsibility to discuss what led me to write about it and what I tried to put into it."

About himself, the 51-year-old DeLillo prefers not to say much. Perhaps fortuitously for a writer who wants to maintain his privacy, an unfinished front stoop has temporarily barred entrance to his Westchester home. In the empty office of a Viking editor on her honeymoon, DeLillo sips Coke from a sweating aluminum can. The white noise of a small fan's whirr is noticeable only during DeLillo's frequent pauses; in conversation as in his novels, he is careful of making language convey his exact meaning. "Whatever there is about language in my work," he says at one point, "it's simply there, it simply seeps out of me and onto the page."

DeLillo says: "I hear voices, I look at faces, and that's always the starting point, and what flows from that, just flows. . . . *Libra* started with my interest in Oswald, what he looked like, what he sounded like, where he lived. I went to Dallas and Fort Worth and New Orleans just to look at houses he lived in. I found it to be a haunting experience. You get a sense of someone who's lived on the margins of history all his life. Sadness and regret and tragedy kind of hovers over these places. . . .

"Eventually," DeLillo says, "a novel begins to reveal its themes to me, but I might be working on it for a year and a half before I have the faintest idea what it eventually is going to be about, what will sail above the heads of the characters, so to speak. . . . That's how I operate as a writer. In *Libra*, something literally sails above the heads of the characters, the U2 plane, which became a kind of unifying element in the book, and which is a sort of token of mystery—and I think can even be seen as part of that current of elements that stand outside history, which David Ferrie [a character in the novel] refers to when he reveals that what [the conspirators want] from Oswald is his participation in an assassination, and he talks about the force of things outside history, the force of dreams, intuitions, prayers, of the effect of the astrological forces of the universe [Libra is Oswald's zodiac sign]. Dreams—that's what this novel is about, it's about history and dreams.

"Coincidence is an important element, like those of dreams and prayers," DeLillo adds. "Coincidence informs the whole novel in a sense. How did Oswald feel when he first found out that the Kennedy motorcade would pass right under his window? That, in addition to the point he had arrived at in his life, had to be one of the powerful motivating elements in his decision to take a shot at Kennedy. This is one of the things I'm talking about when I say 'forces outside of history'—something we don't understand, but which motivates many acts that have changed history. No one has ever been able to find the slightest evidence that Oswald's employment at the Texas School Book Depository was anything but innocent. Nobody placed him there, nobody knew the motorcade would be going that way until a few days before it actually occurred. I suppose this is ultimately why coincidence keeps building in the novel until it finally reaches its grotesque fulfillment."

Within *Libra* and all his other books, DeLillo observes, there is "an element of unresolvability" that reflects the psychic confusion the assassination has precipitated in American life and which is "absolutely . . . where [my work] all began. . . . I don't know exactly how to summarize my work but

I would say it's about danger, modern danger." There are connections between *Libra* and its predecessors, DeLillo says, though the links among his novels "are unconscious because I'm not that aware of what the links are myself, it's just the way my mind works and how I perceive the world."

Either, he hypothesizes, "everything I've done has been building toward this, toward this character in particular; [or] Oswald himself, the assassination itself, was the starting point of my work, although I didn't know it at the time. It's not, I think, that I've been accumulating characters and a particular style and a particular set of experiences that culminate in this novel. It may be that everything I've been doing all along is unwittingly influenced by November 22, and particularly by Oswald. I certainly wasn't aware of it, and I've just begun to think in those terms now, after I've done the novel."

In 1963, DeLillo, who grew up in the Bronx (coincidentally, near where Lee Harvey Oswald once lived, although the two never met), was "working as a copywriter in an ad agency. And that was the next to last year of my advertising career, which was short, uninteresting." Later, as a freelance writer, "I did all sorts of assignments. One day I would be writing about pseudo-colonial furniture, the next day about computers." He began his first novel "around 1966. It took a long time"—*Americana*, in which the assassination figures, was published by Houghton Mifflin in 1971—"because I had to keep interrupting [it] in order to make a living."

Each of his novels, DeLillo says, "is unresolvable, absolutely, and could probably not have been written in the world that existed before the assassination. But I've not been conscious of having been influenced by that event. Still, when people want to know about writers who have influenced other writers, maybe the question ought to be: 'What is there in your life—private or public—that has influenced you?'"

Writing *Libra* took DeLillo three years, from October 1984 to October 1987. "It had never occurred to me before to base a novel on an historic event," he says, "certainly not in a large-scale way. So this novel may in some way be a culmination of ideas in my work, but it also stands a little to the side, because it is so different in that sense and because I was grappling with a real event. It also has had a stronger effect on me for that reason. I'm sure that this novel will be harder to stop thinking about than the others, harder to put into the past and possibly harder to go on from. Surrounded as I am by research materials, in particular by the 26 volumes of the Warren Report, I'll always look at that stuff and think of the strange lonely feeling I had standing in Dealey Plaza one afternoon. A striking sense of mystery, unresolvability, hovers over that little green spot. It seems the loneliest place in the city, even with the cars roaring by constantly. And that's my feeling about the whole experience. I don't think doing a novel about it completes the mystery, not for me, and certainly not for anyone else."

DeLillo says that he "felt a very strong responsibility to fact *where we knew it*. And I made up the rest because we don't know it. If there was a conspiracy, we don't know how it evolved. Oswald is as close as I could make him to what I perceived to be the real person. I really didn't take liberty with fact so much as I invented fresh fact, if you can call it that. I tried very hard to create a unified structure with no seams showing. That was my major technical challenge."

DeLillo depended on the Warren Report and conducted no interviews. He did watch "an extraordinary compilation of amateur footage shot during the motorcade in Dallas [including the Zapruder film as well as other film]. Very crude, powerful footage which as much as anything, I suppose, suggests that the shot that killed Kennedy came from the front instead of from the rear. It's hard seeing that moment of death and blood spurting and then accept the fact that the shot came from the School Book Depository instead of from the grassy knoll. Although I'm sure scientists would find reasons to explain the movement of the president's body, when you see it, it's hard to believe that he wasn't hit from the front. There's no doubt that Oswald hit him, the question is whether he killed him." In *Libra*, Oswald is not a lone gunman.

That the assassination is on film compounds the strangeness of the event and unsettles historical finality: "I think that's one of the things that informed my subsequent work, or all my work," DeLillo says. "The notion of a medium between an event and an audience, film and television in particular. The irony is that we have film of the assassination and yet it is still remote. Because the film is so imperfect. And even if it weren't, I'm sure there are reasons—it's hard not to call them psychological—and anomalies of perception that would still make it difficult to figure out what happened, even if we had expert footage, clear footage, even if we had sound. I think we see different things in the assassination at different periods in our history. We feel a bit differently about it today than we did in the '60s and then in the '70s. But we still don't know what happened, that's the core of it."

DeLillo thinks that "when the authorities quickly determined that Oswald was the lone gunman and an unstable man, people quickly accepted that because it resolved a certain level of anxiety about the very nature of political conspiracy. Some people prefer to believe in conspiracy because they are made anxious by random acts. Believing in conspiracy is almost comforting because, in a sense, a conspiracy is a story we tell each other to ward off the dread of chaotic and random acts. Conspiracy offers coherence.

"The reason so many people think Oswald was not the lone gunman is that the physical evidence, as we know it, argues against it in many respects. But in another way we could interpret the past 25 years as a conspiracy developing in our own minds. Many more people today believe there was a conspiracy than believed it in 1963. Did we invent the conspiracy because it's easier to accept than a random act with no basis in motivation, which is total madness? Is the conspiracy our doing rather than an actual plot against the president's life? That's an unanswerable question," DeLillo acknowledges. "I am suggesting that it is possible to make up stories in order to soothe the dissatisfactions of the past, take the edge off the uncertainties. Perhaps we've invented conspiracies for our own psychic well-being, to heal ourselves."

"An Outsider in This Society": An Interview with Don DeLillo

Anthony DeCurtis / 1988

From *South Atlantic Quarterly*, 89, no.2, 281–304. Expanded from "Matters of Fact and Fiction," *Rolling Stone*, November 17, 1988, pp. 113–122. © Rolling Stone LLC 1988. All rights reserved. Reprinted by permission.

It began like this. In May of 1988 a friend of mine in the publicity department at Viking called and said that Don DeLillo's new novel, *Libra*, about the assassination of President Kennedy, would be published soon, and that, uncharacteristically, DeLillo might be willing to do some interviews. Because DeLillo had written a piece about the assassination for *Rolling Stone* in 1983, my friend thought *Rolling Stone* was one magazine DeLillo might talk to.

I was delighted. I asked him to send along the galleys for the novel, and said I'd bring it up with the magazine's executive editor. The galleys arrived with a note that read, in part, "As I told you over the phone, DeLillo has been very reluctant to give interviews in the past. But with the right person, and with the proper format (one restricting itself mostly to the book itself, and to the life and times of Lee Harvey Oswald), DeLillo might be agreeable. A few biographical details won't hurt, but he's wary of the full treatment."

Everyone at *Rolling Stone* went wild over the book. I wrote my friend that we were willing to do the interview on more or less whatever terms DeLillo stated. He passed our request along to DeLillo. DeLillo turned us down.

I talked to my friend. Would it help if I wrote a letter directly to DeLillo—that is, addressed to DeLillo by name, delivered to my friend to pass along to DeLillo—telling him what the interview would be like and explaining a little bit about myself? It might.

I spent a couple of hours writing the letter. It included earnest sentences like, "In addition to being a senior writer at *Rolling Stone*, I hold a Ph.D. in contemporary fiction from Indiana University, and I'm very familiar with all your novels." It also included a paragraph summary of how I thought *Libra* related to his earlier books, which, with true journalistic economy, I later plumbed for the introduction I wrote for the interview when it eventually ran in *Rolling Stone*.

As I wrote the letter, I was both haunted and inhibited by the references
to journalists in DeLillo's books. It was hard, at least in my own mind, not
to sound like one of his characters. I consciously used the term "full-length
interview" in the letter, rather than the first term that came to mind—
"major piece"—because of a specific passage in which the filmmaker in
The Names speaks about writers: "You know how I am about privacy. I'd
hate to think you came here to do a story on me. A major piece, as
they say. Full of insights. The man and his work. . . . The filmmaker
on location. The filmmaker in seclusion. Major pieces. They're always
major pieces."

Writing for *Rolling Stone* presented complexities along that line as well.
The magazine that gives DeLillo's novel *Running Dog* its title bears some
resemblance to *Rolling Stone*. And, as someone who writes primarily about
rock 'n roll, I've always loved the passage in *Great Jones Street*, in which a television reporter from ABC shows up at the apartment of Bucky Wunderlick,
rock star in self-exile, to ask for an interview:

> "Who are you?"
> "ABC," he said.
> "Forget it."
> "Nothing big or elaborate. An abbreviated interview. Your televised comments on
> topics of interest. Won't take ten minutes. We're all set up downstairs. Ten minutes.
> You've got my word, Bucky. The word of a personal admirer."
> "Positively never."

"I haven't done this kind of massive research since I've been in the glam-
our end of the business," the reporter pleads—a plea ("I'm very familiar with
all your novels") that touches the heart of an exacademic now at play in the
fields of popular culture.

Anyway, I gave the letter to my friend and went on vacation. It was late
June by this time. When I returned around July 4th there was a message on
my answering machine from my friend. "Don liked your letter," he declared.
(Student eternal, I confess to thrilling at the words.) Don—suddenly, now, he
was Don—was more interested in doing the interview; he would call me—
himself!—to discuss it further. If all this sounds protracted and unnecessarily
complicated, you've never tried to get an interview with Sting, David Byrne,
or George Harrison.

One afternoon a few days later, the phone rang at work: "This is Don DeLillo." The questions were simple and friendly: "How do you go about doing one of these things?" (We meet someplace quiet and talk for about two hours with a tape recorder running.) "Do you do much editing?" (Yes, for reasons of space and because a lively spoken conversation does not necessarily translate directly into a lively printed interview. [For the record, all material of interest that was edited out of the interview as it appeared in *Rolling Stone* for reasons of space has been restored for this version.]) "Where do you want to do this?" (Wherever you like that's quiet.) We arranged to meet at his house a few weeks later.

The train ride from midtown Manhattan to the picture-book Westchester suburb where DeLillo lives offers a capsule view of virtually the entire spectrum of American life. After leaving Grand Central Station, the train comes up from underground at Ninety-sixth Street on Manhattan's East Side, rolls serenely through Harlem, them crosses the Harlem River and enters the devastated landscape of the South Bronx. The journey continues through the North Bronx, the working-class neighborhood where DeLillo, whose parents were Italian immigrants, grew up and attended college at Fordham University. Finally, the train passes into Westchester's leafy environs.

At DeLillo's station, the author and his wife, Barbara Bennett, were waiting. The sun was blazing. A crushing August heat. Like the train trip, which links the quotidian splendor and the nightmarish underside of the American dream, the brutal weather seemed appropriate. "This is the last comfortable moment you'll have for a while," DeLillo said with a smile as he got in the car. "The car is air-conditioned, but the house isn't." Bennett, who was driving, jokingly suggested that we do the interview in the car, or perhaps at a local bar. When I told the couple about the hard time I had recently interviewing a musician who was frustratingly inarticulate and far more adept at talking around questions than answering them, DeLillo turned around and assured me, "I plan to be exactly that way myself."

One of the major voices in American fiction for nearly two decades, DeLillo, who is now fifty-one, said he rarely grants interviews because he lacks "the necessary self-importance." "I'm just not a public man," he said. "I'd rather write my books in private and then send them out into the world to discover their own public life.

"*Libra* is easier to talk about than my previous books," he continued. "The obvious reason is it's grounded in reality and there are real people to discuss.

Even someone who hasn't read the book can respond at least in a limited way to any discussion of people like Lee Oswald or Jack Ruby. It is firmer material. I'm always reluctant to get into abstract discussions, which I admit my earlier novels tended to lean toward. I wrote them, but I don't necessarily enjoy talking about them."

Still, *Libra*—DeLillo's ninth novel—is more of a culmination than a departure. DeLillo's first novel, *Americana*, which appeared in 1971, ends in Dealey Plaza, in Dallas, the site of the Kennedy assassination, and references to the slaying turn up in several of his other books. The piece DeLillo wrote for *Rolling Stone* in 1983, "American Blood," effectively serves as a précis for *Libra*.

Moreover, rather than advancing yet another "theory" of the assassination, *Libra* simply carries forward the themes of violence and conspiracy that have come to define DeLillo's fiction. "This is a work of the imagination," he writes in the author's note that concludes the book. "While drawing from the historical record, I've made no attempt to furnish factual answers to any questions raised by the assassination." Instead, he hopes the novel will provide "a way of thinking about the assassination without being constrained by half-facts or overwhelmed by possibilities, by the tide of speculation that widens with the years."

In *Libra*, DeLillo describes the murder of the President as "the seven seconds that broke the back of the American century." But this cataclysm differs only in scale from the killings that shatter complacent, enclosed lives in *Players* (1977), *Running Dog* (1978), and *The Names* (1982). Similarly, the college football player who is the main character in *End Zone* (1972) and the rock-star hero of *Great Jones Street* (1973) both achieve an alienation that rivals the emotional state DeLillo sees in Lee Harvey Oswald. Apocalyptic events profound in their impact and uncertain in their ultimate meaning shadow *Ratner's Star* (1976) and *White Noise* (1985), just as the assassination does the world of *Libra*—and our world, a quarter of a century after it occurred.

The interview took place in DeLillo's backyard; afterward we went off to a diner on the town square—a village center DeLillo approvingly described as "like something out of the fifties"—for a late lunch of burgers, fries, and Cokes. In his yard, DeLillo sat on a lawn chair and sipped iced tea. Fortunately, the yard was shady, and the sky clouded over a bit. Even so, the heat, the humidity, the lush green of the grounds and the eerie din of cicadas gave the scene an almost tropical feel. DeLillo—wiry and intense, wearing jeans and a plaid shirt open at the collar, speaking with deliberate slowness in a gripping monotone—seemed the image of a modern-day Kurtz, a literary explorer of the heart of darkness comfortably at home in the suburbs of America.

DeCurtis: The Kennedy assassination seems perfectly in line with the concerns of your fiction. Do you feel you could have invented it if it hadn't happened?

DeLillo: Maybe it invented me. Certainly, when it happened, I was not a fully formed writer; I had only published some short stories in small quarterlies. As I was working on *Libra*, it occurred to me that a lot of tendencies in my first eight novels seemed to be collecting around the dark center of the assassination. So it's possible I wouldn't have become the kind of writer I am if it weren't for the assassination. Certainly when it happened I had no feeling that it was part of the small universe of my work, because my work, as I say, was completely undeveloped at that point.

DeCurtis: What kind of impact did the assassination have on you?

DeLillo: It had a strong impact, as it obviously did for everyone. As the years have flowed away from that point, I think we've all come to feel that what's been missing over these past twenty-five years is a sense of a manageable reality. Much of that feeling can be traced to that one moment in Dallas. We seem much more aware of elements like randomness and ambiguity and chaos since then.

A character in the novel describes the assassination as "an aberration in the heartland of the real." We still haven't reached any consensus on the specifics of the crime: the number of gunmen, the number of shots, the location of the shots, the number of wounds in the President's body—the list goes on and on. Beyond this confusion of data, people have developed a sense that history has been secretly manipulated. Documents lost and destroyed. Official records sealed for fifty or seventy-five years. A number of suggestive murders and suicides involving people who were connected to the events of November 22nd. So from the initial impact of the visceral shock, I think we've developed a much more deeply unsettled feeling about our grip on reality.

DeCurtis: You have been interested for a long time in the media, which certainly played a major role in the national experience of the assassination. Television had just made its impact on politics in the 1960 election, and then for the week following the murder, it seemed that everyone was watching television, seeing Jack Ruby's murder of Lee Harvey Oswald and then Kennedy's funeral. It's as if the power of the media in our culture hadn't been fully felt until that point.

DeLillo: It's strange that the power of television was utilized to its fullest, perhaps for the first time, as it pertained to a violent event. Not only a violent, but, of course, an extraordinarily significant event. This has become part of our consciousness. We've developed almost a sense of performance as it applies to televised events. And I think some of the people who are essential to such events—particularly violent events and particularly people like Arthur Bremer and John Hinckley—are simply carrying their performing selves out of the wings and into the theater. Such young men have a sense of the way in which their acts will be perceived by the rest of us, even as they commit the acts. So there is a deeply self-referential element in our lives that wasn't there before.

DeCurtis: The inevitable question: Where were you when John Kennedy was shot?

DeLillo: I was eating lunch with two friends in a restaurant on the west side of Manhattan and actually heard about the shooting at a bank a little later. I overheard a bank teller telling a customer that the President had been shot in Dallas. And my first curious reaction was, "I didn't even know he was in Dallas." Obviously it was totally beside the point. But the small surprise then, of course, yielded to the enormous shock of what these words meant. I didn't watch very much television that weekend. I didn't watch much of the funeral. I think I have a kind of natural antipathy to formal events of that kind. But certainly a sense of death seemed to permeate everything for the next four or five days.

DeCurtis: You refer to the assassination at various points in novels prior to *Libra*, and of course you wrote an essay about the assassination for *Rolling Stone* in 1983. What finally made you feel that you had to pursue it as the subject of a novel?

DeLillo: I didn't start thinking about it as a major subject until the early part of this decade. When I did the 1983 piece in *Rolling Stone*, I began to realize how enormously wide-reaching the material was and how much more deeply I would have to search before I could begin to do justice to it. Because I'm a novelist, I guess I defined "justice" in terms of a much more full-bodied work than the nonfiction piece I had done, and so I began to think seriously about a novel.

Possibly a motivating element was the fact that Oswald and I lived within six or seven blocks of each other in the Bronx. I didn't know this until I did the research for the *Rolling Stone* piece. He and his mother, Marguerite, traveled to New York in '52 or early '53, because her oldest son was stationed at Ellis Island with the Coast Guard. They got in the car and drove all the way to New York and eventually settled in the Bronx. Oswald lived very near the Bronx Zoo. I guess he was thirteen and I was sixteen at the time. I suppose this gave me a personal nudge toward the material.

Turning it into fiction brought a number of issues to the surface. If I make an extended argument in the book it's not that the assassination necessarily happened this way. The argument is that this is an interesting way to write fiction about a significant event that happens to have these general contours and these agreed-upon characters. It's my feeling that readers will accept or reject my own variations on the story based on whether these things work as fiction, not whether they coincide with the reader's own theories or the reader's own memories. So this is the path I had to drive through common memory and common history to fiction.

DeCurtis: Did it seem odd that some reviews evaluated your theory of the assassination almost as if it were fact and not fiction?
DeLillo: Inevitably some people reviewed the assassination itself, instead of a piece of work which is obviously fiction. My own feeling at the very beginning was that I had to do justice to historical likelihood. In other words, I chose what I consider the most obvious possibility: that the assassination was the work of anti-Castro elements. I could perhaps have written the same book with a completely different assassination scenario. I wanted to be obvious in this case because I didn't want novelistic invention to become the heart of the book. I wanted a clear historical center on which I could work my fictional variations.

DeCurtis: Apart from the personal reason you mentioned, why did you choose to tell the story from Oswald's point of view?

DeLillo: I think I have an idea of what it's like to be an outsider in this society. Oswald was clearly an outsider, although he fought against his exclusion. I had a very haunting sense of what kind of life he led and what kind of person he was. I experienced it when I saw the places where he lived in New Orleans and in Dallas and in Fort Worth. I had a very clear sense of a man living on the margins of society. He was the kind of person we think we know until we delve more deeply. Who would have expected someone like that to defect to the Soviet Union? He started reading socialist writing when he was fifteen; then, as soon as he became old enough, joined the Marines. This element of self-contradiction seemed to exemplify his life. There seemed to be a pattern of self-argument.

When he returned from the Soviet Union, he devised a list of answers to possible questions he'd be asked by the authorities upon disembarking. One set of answers could be characterized as the replies of a simple tourist who just happened to have spent two-and-a-half years at the heart of the Soviet Union and is delighted to be returning to his home country. The other set of answers was full of defiance and anger at the inequities of life in capitalist society. It carried a strong sense of his refusal to explain why he left this country to settle in Russia. These mutually hostile elements seemed always to be part of Oswald's life, and, I think, separate him slightly from the general run of malcontents and disaffected people.

DeCurtis: It's almost as if Oswald embodied a postmodern notion of character in which the self isn't fixed and you assume or discard traits as the mood strikes you.

DeLillo: Someone who knew Oswald referred to him as an actor in real life, and I do think there is a sense in which he was watching himself perform. I tried to insert this element into *Libra* on a number of occasions.

I think Oswald anticipates men like Hinckley and Bremer. His attempt to kill General Edwin Walker was a strictly political act: Walker was a right-wing figure, and Oswald was, of course, pro-Castro. But Oswald's attempt on Kennedy was more complicated. I think it was based on elements outside politics and, as someone in the novel says, outside history—things like dreams and coincidences and even the movement or the configuration of the stars, which is one reason the book is called *Libra*. The rage and frustration he had felt for twenty-four years, plus the enormous coincidence that the motorcade would be passing the building where he worked—these are the things that combined to drive Oswald toward attempting to kill the President. So in this second murder attempt I think he presages the acts of all of the subsequent disaffected young men who seem to approach their assassination attempts out of a backdrop of dreams and personal fantasy much more than politics.

DeCurtis: You quote Oswald's statement about wanting to be a fiction writer, and you describe him as having lived a life in small rooms, which is a phrase similar to ones you've used to describe your life as a writer. Do you see Oswald as an author of some kind?

DeLillo: Well, he did make that statement in his application for the Albert Schweitzer College. He did say he wanted to be a writer. He wanted to write "short stories on contemporary American life"—and this, of course, is a striking remark coming from someone like him. There's no evidence that he ever wrote any fiction; none apparently survived if he did. But I think the recurring motif in the book of men in small rooms refers to Oswald much more as an outsider than as a writer. I think he had a strong identification with people like Trotsky and Castro, who spent long periods in prison. I think he felt that with enough perseverance and enough determination these men would survive their incarcerations and eventually be swept by history right out of the room. Out of the room and out of the *self*. To merge with history is to escape the self. I think Oswald knew this. He said as much in a letter to his brother. It is the epigraph [to *Libra*]: "Happiness is taking part in the struggle, where there is no borderline between one's own personal world, and the world in general."

I think we can take Oswald's life as the attempt to find that place. But he never could. He never lost sight of the borderline. He never was able to merge with the world in general or with history in particular. His life in small rooms is the antithesis of the life America seems to promise its citizens: the life of consumer fulfillment. And I think it's interesting that a man like Oswald would return to this country from Russia with a woman who, of course and understandably, was completely amazed by this world of American consumer promise. I think it must have caused an enormous tension in his life. Her desire to become more fully a part of this paradise she'd been hearing about all her life and his ambivalent feelings about being a husband who provides for his family and at the same time being a leftist who finds an element of distaste in consumer fulfillment. In one of his apartments in Dallas he actually worked in a room almost the size of a closet. This seemed almost the kind of negative culmination of a certain stream that was running through my own work of men finding themselves alone in small rooms. And here is a man, and not even a man I invented, a real man who finds himself in a closet-sized room planning the murder of General Walker.

DeCurtis: You read the Warren Commission Report and traveled quite a bit. Did you do other research for *Libra*?
DeLillo: I looked at films and listened to tapes. Hearing Oswald's voice and his mother's voice was extremely interesting. Particularly interesting was a tape of an appearance Oswald made on the radio in New Orleans in the summer of 1963. He sounds like a socialist candidate for office. He was extremely articulate and extremely clever in escaping difficult questions. Listening to this man and then reading the things he had earlier written in his so-called historic diary, which is enormously chaotic and almost childlike, again seemed to point to a man who was a living self-contradiction. Nothing I had earlier known about Oswald led me to think that he could sound so intelligent and articulate as he did on this radio program.

The movie I looked at is a compilation of amateur footage taken that day in Dallas, and it covers a period from the time the President's plane landed in Dallas until the assassination itself. It's extremely crude footage, but all the more powerful because of it. I suppose the most powerful moment is also the most ambiguous. We see the shot that kills the President, but it seems to be surrounded in chaos and in shadow and in blurs. The strongest feeling I took away from that moment is the feeling that the shot came from the front and not from the rear. Of course, if that's true, there had to be more than one assassin. In fact, it's hard to escape that feeling. The other strange moment, I suppose, is when dozens and dozens of people are seen shortly after the shooting running up a set of stairs that proceeds right toward the grassy knoll and toward the stockade fence which separated Dealey Plaza from a parking lot. I hadn't read in any earlier accounts that there had been such an exodus from the scene, and seeing it was shocking because it seemed to indicate that people were running in the direction they thought the shots had come from, not just four or five people, but possibly as many as fifty. And it's just another of those mysteries that hovers over the single moment of death.

DeCurtis: At one point you describe the Warren Commission Report, which is twenty-six volumes long, as the novel that James Joyce might have written if he had moved to Iowa City and lived to be a hundred.

DeLillo: I asked myself what Joyce could possibly do after *Finnegans Wake*, and this was the answer. It's an amazing document. The first fifteen volumes are devoted to testimony and the last eleven volumes to exhibits, and together we have a masterwork of trivia ranging from Jack Ruby's mother's dental records to photographs of knotted string. What was valuable to me most specifically was the testimony of dozens and dozens of people who talk not only about their connection to the assassination itself but about their jobs, their marriages, their children. This testimony provided an extraordinary window on life in the fifties and sixties and, beyond that, gave me a sense of people's speech patterns, whether they were private detectives from New Orleans or railroad workers from Fort Worth. I'm sure that without those twenty-six volumes I would have written a very different novel and probably a much less interesting one.

DeCurtis: How long did it take to write *Libra*?

DeLillo: A little over three years. The only time I had to do this much research was in writing *Ratner's Star*. But I found doing this novel much more invigorating, I think because the reading I had to do dealt with real people and not with science and mathematics and astronomy and so on. And for the same reason I'm sure the experience of writing this novel will stay with me much longer. In fact, I'm certain I'll never quite get rid of these characters and this story. They'll always be part of my life.

DeCurtis: What was your writing regimen once you started working on the book?

DeLillo: Well this book is unusual in my own experience because I worked two sessions a day at the typewriter, and this is the first time I've ever done that for an extended period. I worked in the morning, roughly from nine to one, and then again in early evening for about an hour and a half. I couldn't do all the research, all the reading, in one extended stretch and then begin to write the novel, because there was simply too much reading to do. So I had to space it chronologically. This meant that often I worked much of the day at the typewriter and then spent the night or part of the night trying to catch up. One week I'd be exploring the Bay of Pigs, the next week the Italian mafia and the next week the Yuri Nosenko affair and the next week the U-2 incident. So I felt that I had to write nearly twice as much in a given day just to keep up.

DeCurtis: Given the complexity of the subject, was there any point that constituted a breakthrough for you?
DeLillo: Once I found Oswald's voice—and by voice I mean not just the way he spoke to people but his inner structure, his consciousness, the sound of his thinking—I began to feel that I was nearly home free. It's interesting that once you find the right rhythm for your sentences, you may be well on your way to finding the character himself. And once I came upon a kind of abrupt, broken rhythm both in dialogue and in narration, I felt this was the prose counterpart to not only Oswald's inner life but Jack Ruby's as well. And other characters too. So the prose itself began to suggest not the path the novel would take but the deepest motivation of the characters who originated this prose in a sense.

DeCurtis: The title *Libra* seems to reflect the concern in your novels with the occult and superstitions of various kinds. What fascinates you about those nonrational systems?
DeLillo: I think my work has always been informed by mystery; the final answer, if there is one at all, is outside the book. My books are open-ended. I would say that mystery in general rather than the occult is something that weaves in and out of my work. I can't tell you where it came from or what it leads to. Possibly it is the natural product of a Catholic upbringing.
Libra was Oswald's sign, and because Libra refers to the scales, it seemed appropriate to a man who harbored contradictions and who could tilt either way.

DeCurtis: Did you consider other titles?
DeLillo: The first title I considered was the one I used for the *Rolling Stone* piece, "American Blood." As the months passed, I think the only other title that interested me as I went along was "Texas School Book," which seemed to have a sort of double resonance. It was, of course, the Texas School Book Depository where Oswald worked, and the notion of schoolbooks seemed relevant to his life and his struggle. But finally when I hit upon this notion of coincidence and dream and intuition and the possible impact of astrology on

the way men act, I thought that Libra, being Oswald's sign, would be the one title that summarized what's inside the book.

DeCurtis: Did you select the photo of Oswald that's on the cover?
DeLillo: I asked Viking to consider using it, yes. It seems that picture would be one of the central artifacts of Oswald's life. He is holding a rifle, carrying a revolver at his hip and holding in his free hand copies of *The Militant* and *The Worker*, two left-wing journals he regularly read. He's dressed in black. He's almost the poor man's James Dean in that picture, and there's definitely an idea of the performing self. He told his wife that he wanted her to take this picture so that their daughter may one day know what kind of person her father was.

DeCurtis: In the author's note at the end of *Libra*, you say the novel might serve as a kind of refuge for readers. There is an implication that searching for a "solution" to the mysteries of the assassination, as the CIA historian Nicholas Branch does in the book, leads inevitably to a mental and spiritual dead end. What does fiction offer people that history denies to them?
DeLillo: Branch feels overwhelmed by the massive data he has to deal with. He feels the path is changing as he writes. He despairs of being able to complete a coherent account of this extraordinarily complex event. I think the fiction writer tries to redeem this despair. Stories can be a consolation—at least in theory. The novelist can try to leap across the barrier of fact, and the reader is willing to take that leap with him as long as there's a kind of redemptive truth waiting on the other side, a sense that we've arrived at a resolution.

I think fiction rescues history from its confusions. It can do this in the somewhat superficial way of filling in blank spaces. But it also can operate in a deeper way: providing the balance and rhythm we don't experience in our daily lives, in our real lives. So the novel which is within history can also operate outside it—correcting, clearing up and, perhaps most important of all, finding rhythms and symmetries that we simply don't encounter elsewhere. If *Ratner's Star* is, in part, a way to embody what it is all about, that is, if it's a book of harmonies and symmetries, because mathematics is a search for a sense of order in our lives, then I think *Libra* is, in a curious way, related to *Ratner's Star*, because it attempts to provide a hint of order in the midst of all the randomness.

DeCurtis: Do you see the book as related in any way to other novels about public events, like Norman Mailer's *The Executioner's Song*, which is about the execution of Gary Gilmore, or Robert Coover's *The Public Burning*, about the Rosenbergs?

DeLillo: I haven't thought about *Libra* in terms of other novels at all—including the so-called nonfiction novels, like *In Cold Blood* or *The Armies of the Night*. It doesn't seem to me to be part of the same current of contemporary fiction. I think of it as a novel. And as I was trying to explain earlier, I think that the book is an exploration of what variations we might take on an actual event rather than an argument that this is what really happened in Dallas in November of 1963 and in the months before and in the years that have followed.

DeCurtis: From a certain vantage point, your books can almost be taken as a systematic look at various aspects of American life: the Kennedy assassination; rock music in *Great Jones Street*; science and mathematics in *Ratner's Star*; football in *End Zone*. Do you proceed in that methodical a fashion?

DeLillo: No, not at all. That notion breaks down rather easily if you analyze it. *Americana* is not about any one area of our experience. *End Zone* wasn't about football. It's a fairly elusive novel. It seems to me to be about extreme places and extreme states of mind, more than anything else. Certainly there is very little about rock music in *Great Jones Street*, although the hero is a musician. The interesting thing about that particular character is that he seems to be at a crossroad between murder and suicide. For me, that defines the period between 1965 and 1975, say, and I thought it was best exemplified in a rock-music star. *Ratner's Star* is not about mathematics as such. I've never attempted to embark on a systematic exploration of American experience. I take the ideas as they come.

DeCurtis: On the other hand, some specific American realities have a draw for you.

DeLillo: Certainly there are themes that recur. Perhaps a sense of secret patterns in our lives. A sense of ambiguity. Certainly the violence of contemporary life is a motif. I see contemporary violence as a kind of sardonic response to the promise of consumer fulfillment in America. Again we come back to these men in small rooms who can't get out and who have to organize their desperation and their loneliness, who have to give it a destiny and who often end up doing this through violent means. I see this desperation against the backdrop of brightly colored packages and products and consumer happiness and every promise that American life makes day by day and minute by minute everywhere we go.

DeCurtis: In *The Names*, which is principally set in Greece, you speak about the way Americans abroad especially seem to feel the imminence of violence.
DeLillo: I do believe that Americans living abroad feel a self-consciousness that they don't feel when they are at home. They become students of themselves. They see themselves as the people around them see them, as Americans with a capital A. Because being American is a sensitive thing in so many parts of the world, the American response to violence, to terror, in places like the Middle East and Greece is often a response tinged with inevitability, almost with apology. We're just waiting for it to happen to us. It becomes part of a sophisticated form of humor that people exchange almost as a matter of course. The humor of political dread.

DeCurtis: Humor plays an important role in your novels. Do you see it as providing relief from the grimness of some of your subjects?
DeLillo: I don't think the humor is intended to counteract the fear. It's almost part of it. We ourselves may almost instantaneously use humor to offset a particular moment of discomfort or fear, but this reflex is so deeply woven into the original fear that they almost become the same thing.

DeCurtis: Your first novel, *Americana*, was published when you were about thirty-five, which is rather late. Did you think of yourself as a writer before that?
DeLillo: *Americana* took a long time to write because I had to keep interrupting it to earn a living, which I was doing at that time by writing freelance, mostly advertising material. It also took a long time because I didn't know what I was doing. I was about two years into the novel when I realized I was a writer—not because I thought the novel would even be published but because sentence by sentence and paragraph by paragraph I was beginning to see that I had abilities I hadn't demonstrated in earlier work, that is, in short stories I'd written when I was younger. I had a feeling that I could not solve the structural problems in *Americana*, but it didn't disturb me. Once I realized that I was good enough to be a professional writer, I simply kept

going in the somewhat blind belief that nature would eventually take its course.

I think I started work on *End Zone* just weeks after I finished *Americana*. The long-drawn-out, somewhat aimless experience of writing *Americana* was immediately replaced by a quick burst of carefully directed activity. I did *End Zone* in about one-fourth the time it had taken me to write *Americana*.

DeCurtis: At what point were you able to earn your living as a fiction writer?
DeLillo: Starting with *End Zone*, I stopped doing every other kind of writing.

DeCurtis: Movies frequently come up in your work. When did they become significant for you?
DeLillo: I began to understand the force that movies could have emotionally and intellectually in what I consider the great era of the European films: Godard, Antonioni, Fellini, Bergman. And American directors as well— Kubrick and Howard Hawks and others.

DeCurtis: What did you find inspirational about those directors?
DeLillo: Well, they seem to fracture reality. They find mystery in common-place moments. They find humor in even the gravest political acts. They seem to find an art and a seriousness which I think was completely unexpected and which had once been the province of literature alone. So that a popular art was suddenly seen as a serious art. And this was interesting and inspiring.

DeCurtis: Both *The Names* and *Ratner's Star* are pretty exacting texts. Is the difficulty of those books part of a commitment you feel you need to demand from readers?
DeLillo: From this perspective I can see that the reader would have to earn his way into *Ratner's Star*, but this was not something I'd been trying to do. I did not have a clear sense of how difficult this book might turn out to be. I just followed my idea chapter by chapter and character by character. It seems to me that *Ratner's Star* is a book which is almost all structure. The structure of the book *is* the book. The characters are intentionally flattened and cartoonlike. I was trying to build a novel which was not only about mathematics

to some extent but which itself would become a piece of mathematics. It would be a book which embodied pattern and order and harmony, which is one of the traditional goals of pure mathematics.

In *The Names*, I spent a lot of time searching for the kind of sun-cut precision I found in Greek light and in the Greek landscape. I wanted a prose which would have the clarity and the accuracy which the natural environment at its best in that part of the world seems to inspire in our own senses. I mean, there were periods in Greece when I tasted and saw and heard with much more sharpness and clarity than I'd ever done before or since. And I wanted to discover a sentence, a way of writing sentences that would be the prose counterpart to that clarity—that sensuous clarity of the Aegean experience. Those were my conscious goals in those two books.

DeCurtis: It's rather uncommon for contemporary writers not to give readings or teach. Why don't you do those things?
DeLillo: Well, the simplest answer is the true one: I never liked school. Why go back now? I simply never wanted to teach. I never felt I had anything worth saying to students. I felt that whatever value my work has is something of a mystery to me. Although I could discuss with limited success what devices I've used to build certain structures in my books, I wouldn't know how to help other writers fulfill their own visions. And besides I'm lazy.

DeCurtis: Do you have a sense, because of the extreme issues raised in your work, that one part of your readership is drawn from the fringes of American society?
DeLillo: Yeah, one segment of my readership is marginal, but beyond that I find it hard to analyze the mail I get and make any conclusions as to what kind of readers I have. Certainly, *White Noise* found a lot of women readers, and I don't think too many women had been reading my books before that. So I really can't generalize. In the past I got a lot of letters from people who seemed slightly unbalanced. This hasn't been happening for the past three or four years. It seems that the eighties have been somewhat more sane than the seventies, based on my own limited experience of measuring letters from readers. I've reached no conclusion about the kind of readers I have based on the mail I get. There are all sorts.

DeCurtis: In *The Names* and some of your other books, language itself seems to be one of your subjects. That self-referential quality parallels a lot of theoretical work being done in philosophy and literary criticism these days. Do you read much writing of that kind?

DeLillo: No, I don't. It is just my sense that we live in a kind of circular or near-circular system and that there are an increasing number of rings which keep intersecting at some point, whether you're using a plastic card to draw money out of your account at an automatic teller machine or thinking about the movement of planetary bodies. I mean, these systems all seem to interact to me. But I view all this in the most general terms, and I have no idea what kind of scientific studies are taking place. The secrets within systems, I suppose, are things that have informed my work. But they're almost secrets of consciousness, or ways in which consciousness is replicated in the natural world.

DeCurtis: There also seems to be a fascination with euphemism and jargon in your books; for example, the poisonous cloud of gas that creates an environmental disaster in *White Noise* is repeatedly referred to as the "airborne toxic event."

DeLillo: It's a language that almost holds off reality while at the same time trying to fit it into a formal pattern. The interesting thing about jargon is that if it lives long enough, it stops being jargon and becomes part of natural speech, and we all find ourselves using it. I think we might all be disposed to use phrases like "time frame," which, when it was first used during the Watergate investigation, had an almost evil aura to it, because it was uttered by men we had learned to distrust so deeply.

I don't think of language in a theoretical way. I approach it at street level. That is, I listen carefully to the way people speak. And I find that the closer a writer comes to portraying actual speech, the more stylized it seems on the page, so that the reader may well conclude that this is a formal experiment in dialogue instead of a simple transcription, which it actually is. When I started writing *Players*, my idea was to fill the novel with the kind of intimate, casual, off-the-cuff speech between close friends or husbands and wives. This was the whole point of the book as far as I was concerned. But somehow I got sidetracked almost immediately and found myself describing a murder on the floor of the stock exchange, and of course from that point the book took a completely different direction. Nevertheless, in *Players*, I think there is still a sense of speech as it actually falls from the lips of people. And I did that again in *Libra*. In this case I wasn't translating spoken speech as much as the printed speech of people who testified before the Warren Commission. Marguerite Oswald has an extremely unique way of speaking, and I didn't have to invent this at all. I simply had to read it and then remake it, rehear it for the purposes of the particular passage I was writing.

DeCurtis: Often your characters are criticized for being unrealistic—children who speak like adults or, as in *Ratner's Star*, characters whose consciousnesses seem at points to blur one into the other. How do you view your characters?
DeLillo: Probably *Libra* is the exception to my work in that I tried a little harder to connect motivation with action. This is because there is an official record—if not of motivation, at least of action on the part of so many characters in the book. So it had to make a certain amount of sense, and what sense was missing I tried to supply. For example, why did Oswald shoot President Kennedy? I don't think anyone knows, but in the book I've attempted to fill in that gap, although not at all in a specific way.

There's no short answer to the question. You either find yourself entering a character's life and consciousness or you don't, and in much modern fiction I don't think you are required to, either as a writer or a reader. Many modern characters have a flattened existence—purposely—and many modern characters exist precisely nowhere. There isn't a strong sense of place in much modern writing. Again, this is where I differ from what we could call the mainstream. I do feel a need and a drive to paint a kind of thick surface around my characters. I think all my novels have a strong sense of place.

But in contemporary writing in general, there's a strong sense that the world of Beckett and Kafka has redescended on contemporary America, because characters seem to live in a theoretical environment rather than a real one. I haven't felt that I'm part of that. I've always had a grounding in the real world, whatever esoteric flights I might indulge in from time to time.

DeCurtis: There seems to be a fondness in your writing, particularly in *White Noise*, for what might be described as the trappings of suburban middle-class existence, to the point where one of the characters describes the supermarket as a sacred place.
DeLillo: I would call it a sense of the importance of daily life and of ordinary moments. In *White Noise*, in particular, I tried to find a kind of radiance in

dailiness. Sometimes this radiance can be almost frightening. Other times it can be almost holy or sacred. Is it really there? Well, yes. You know, I don't believe as Murray Jay Siskind does in *White Noise* that the supermarket is a form of Tibetan lamasery. But there is something there that we tend to miss.

Imagine someone from the third world who has never set foot in a place like that suddenly transported to an A&P in Chagrin Falls, Ohio. Wouldn't he be elated or frightened? Wouldn't he sense that something transcending is about to happen to him in the midst of all this brightness? So I think that's something that has been in the background of my work: a sense of something extraordinary hovering just beyond our touch and just beyond our vision.

DeCurtis: Hitler and the Holocaust have repeatedly been addressed in your books. In *Running Dog*, a pornographic movie allegedly filmed in Hitler's bunker determines a good deal of the novel's plot. In *White Noise*, university professor Jack Gladney attempts to calm his obsessive fear of death through his work in the Department of Hitler Studies.

DeLillo: In his case, Gladney finds a perverse form of protection. The damage caused by Hitler was so enormous that Gladney feels he can disappear inside it and that his own puny dread will be over-whelmed by the vastness, the monstrosity of Hitler himself. He feels that Hitler is not only bigger than life, as we say of many famous figures, but bigger than death. Our sense of fear—we avoid it because we feel it so deeply, so there is an intense conflict at work. I brought this conflict to the surface in the shape of Jack Gladney.

I think it is something we all feel, something we almost never talk about, something that is *almost* there. I tried to relate it in *White Noise* to this other sense of transcendence that lies just beyond our touch. This extraordinary wonder of things is somehow related to the extraordinary dread, to the death fear we try to keep beneath the surface of our perceptions.

DeCurtis: What was the idea in *Running Dog* of locating the pornographic movie in Hitler's bunker?

DeLillo: Well, this made it an object of ultimate desirability and ultimate dread, simply because it connected to Hitler. When the Hitler diaries "surfaced," in quotes, in the early eighties, there was even a more beserk reaction to them than there was to this film in *Running Dog*. If anything, I was slightly innocent about my sense of what would happen if such an object emerged.

What I was really getting at in *Running Dog* was a sense of the terrible
acquisitiveness in which we live, coupled with a final indifference to the
object. After all the mad attempts to acquire the thing, everyone suddenly
decides that, well, maybe we really don't care about this so much anyway.
This was something I felt characterized our lives at the time the book was
written, in the mid to late seventies. I think this was part of American
consciousness then.

DeCurtis: What about the fascination with children in your books?
DeLillo: Well, I think we feel, perhaps superstitiously, that children have a
direct route to, have direct contact to the kind of natural truth that eludes us
as adults. In *The Names* the father is transported by what he sees as a kind of
deeper truth underlying the language his son uses in writing his stories. He
sees misspellings and misused words as reflecting a kind of reality that he as
an adult couldn't possibly grasp. And I think he relates this to the practice
of speaking in tongues, which itself is what we might call an alternate reality.
It's a fabricated language which seems to have a certain pattern to it. It isn't
just gibberish. It isn't language, but it isn't gibberish either. And I think this is
the way Axton felt about his own son's writing. And I think this is the way we
feel about children in general. There is something they know but can't tell us.
Or there is something they remember which we've forgotten.
      Glossolalia or speaking in tongues, you know, could be viewed as a higher
form of infantile babbling. It's babbling which seems to mean something,
and this is intriguing.

DeCurtis: *Ratner's Star*, which has a child as its central character, seems to
juxtapose the intense rationality of science with a variety of mystical experiences, like speaking in tongues.
DeLillo: Well, *Ratner's Star* is almost a study of opposites, yes. Only because
I think anyone who studies the history of mathematics finds that the link
between the strictest scientific logic and other mysticism seems to exist.
I mean, this is something any true scientist might tend to deny, but so many
mathematicians, in earlier centuries anyway, were mystical about numbers,
about the movements of heavenly bodies and so forth, while at the same time
being accomplished scientists. And this strange connection of opposites
found its way into *Ratner's Star*. I think modern physicists seem to be moving
toward nearly mystical explanations of the ways in which elements in the

subatomic world and in the galaxy operate. There seems to be something happening.

DeCurtis: You've been denounced as a member of the paranoid left. Do you have a sense of your books as political?
DeLillo: No, I don't. Politics plays a part in some of my books, but this is usually because the characters are political. I don't have a political theory or doctrine that I'm espousing. *Libra* obviously is saturated with politics, of necessity. Certainly the left-wing theories of Oswald do not coincide with my own. I don't have a program. I follow characters where they take me and I don't know what I can say beyond that.

DeCurtis: How do you assess your own works? Are there specific ones that you feel are your best or your favorites?
DeLillo: My feeling is that the novels I've written in the 1980s—*The Names, White Noise,* and *Libra*—are stronger books than the six novels I published in the seventies. This may be what every writer feels about more recent works. But I think the three novels I've written in this decade were more deeply motivated and required a stronger sense of commitment than some of the books I wrote earlier, like, for example, *Running Dog* and possibly *Great Jones Street,* which I think I set out to write because I had become anxious about the amount of time that had passed since I finished my previous book and I wanted to get back to work. I think one of the things I've learned through experience is that it isn't enough to want to get back to work. The other thing I've learned is that no amount of experience can prevent you from making a major mistake. I think it can help you avoid small mistakes. But the potential for a completely misconceived book still exists.

DeCurtis: There's something of an apocalyptic feel about your books, an intimation that our world is moving toward greater randomness and dissolution, or maybe even cataclysm. Do you see this process as irreversible?
DeLillo: It could change tomorrow. This is the shape my books take because this is the reality I see. This reality has become part of all our lives over the past twenty-five years. I don't know how we can deny it.

I don't think *Libra* is a paranoid book at all. I think it's a clear-sighted, reasonable piece of work which takes into account the enormous paranoia which has ensued from the assassination. I can say the same thing about some of my other books. They're *about* movements or feelings in the air and in the culture around us, without necessarily being *part* of the particular movement. I mean, what I sense is suspicion and distrust and fear, and so, of course, these things inform my books. It's my idea of myself as a writer—perhaps mistaken—that I enter these worlds as a completely rational person who is simply taking what he senses all around him and using it as material.

DeCurtis: You've spoken of the redemptive quality of fiction. Do you see your books as offering an alternative to the dark reality you detect?
DeLillo: Well, strictly in theory, art is one of the consolation prizes we receive for having lived in a difficult and sometimes chaotic world. We seek pattern in art that eludes us in natural experience. This isn't to say that art has to be comforting; obviously, it can be deeply disturbing. But nothing in *Libra* can begin to approach the level of disquiet and dread characterized by the assassination itself.

Dangerous Don DeLillo

Vince Passaro / 1991

From *The New York Times Magazine*, May 19, 1991, pp. 34–36, 38, 76–77.
© 1991 by Vince Passaro. Reprinted by permission of Denise Shannon
Literary Agency.

Until 1985, when *White Noise*, his eighth novel, won the National Book
Award, Don DeLillo was something of a cipher. He had for years been the
kind of writer whose books commanded front-page reviews but still managed not to sell. He was well known in literary circles, and to a small, devoted
following, but the chiseled sentences and prescient terrors of his fiction made
him difficult to promote. His work seemed privy to a flow of recent history
that had been obscured from the rest of us—DeLillo had important information about the tenor of our national life, information that we had been feeling in our bones but that he had hardened into words. Yet, for all DeLillo
seemed to know, no one knew much about him. His books, though pro-
foundly political, presented no clear agenda, no comfortably familiar social
world or class of characters. Reading his novels in the 70's and early 80's, I
started to wonder, Who is this guy? The biographical information at the
backs of his books gave only a list of his other titles, with the acknowledge-
ment "He lives in New York City." Occasionally it said "Don DeLillo lives in
New York City" first, then gave the other titles—no writing program he'd
attended, no university where he taught, no mention of whether he had kids
or a dog. Inside, no epigraphs, no effusive thankyous to agents or editors,
friends or neighbors, librarians or auto mechanics.

　　Like Bill Gray, the fictional novelist at the center of his newest book, *Mao
II* (to be published next month by Viking), DeLillo kept himself aloof from
the public ceremonies of authorship. In 1979, he gave a rare interview to a
critic, Tom LeClair, in which LeClair questioned him about what was then
his intriguing absence from the usual authorial rolls. Why all the mystery?
LeClair asked. Why was there so little information extant about him?

　　DeLillo's answer is illuminating. "Silence, exile, cunning and so on," he
said. "It's my nature to keep quiet about most things. Even the ideas in my
work. When you try to unravel something you've written, you belittle it in a
way. It was created as a mystery, in part. Here is a new map of the world; it is

seven shades of blue. If you're able to be straightforward and penetrating about this invention of yours, it's almost as though you're saying it wasn't altogether necessary. The sources weren't deep enough."

When I came upon this interview in 1985, my sense of how a writer pursues a career had been transformed by the 80's spectacle—by the young celebrities, the hard-soft deals and movie contracts, the superagents and media wizardry that were the new ritual and clergy of art's true faith. DeLillo's response yanked me back into real time. It evoked the artistic strategy Stephen Dedalus developed in Joyce's *Portrait of the Artist as a Young Man* ("I will try to express myself in some mode of life or art as freely as I can and as wholly as I can, using for my defence the only arms I allow myself to use— silence, exile and cunning"). More than any other contemporary American writer, DeLillo struck me as fierce and lasting in his importance. His fiction bears down with unnerving humor and unalleviated intelligence and force. As his answer to LeClair makes clear, DeLillo aims to put behind his every lean sentence the power of an extraordinary commitment.

DeLillo is a star now, no longer the shrouded, elusive figure he had been when he was interviewed by LeClair. He does readings from time to time; on rare occasions, he speaks to the press. When I call to make arrangements to discuss *Mao II*, he is cheerful and cooperative. He lives in Westchester these days, but he still spends a good deal of time in the city. He suggests we meet at a restaurant just off Columbus Avenue, an establishment that is, as he puts it, "invariably deserted." He means that it will be an appropriate place for taping, but one senses a deeper satisfaction with the idea.

In person he is reserved and quiet, a nice and gentle man. Our talk ranges over a number of literary and cultural topics besides his work, and several times he offers to send me articles and books that I may not be able to find. His hair, once dark, has turned mostly gray. He is one of those people, invariably intelligent, who seem to live in their eyes—the rest of his face and body don't move much or give anything away. He speaks without inflection, in long and almost perfectly composed sentences. His words issue; you feel he doesn't let them get away without a good deal of relish and a tinge of regret. At the same time, he is friendly and interested, eager to discuss books and questions of sentences and form, generous and admiring of other writers, some of them young and little known.

And yet there is also between us a tangible distance, part of which, no doubt, has to do with the false intimacy that interviews try to force on their participants and that DeLillo will have no part of. He will not spill his guts, you sense, because his guts are reserved for his work. Distance in a writer of DeLillo's acuity is a lifelong habit and need—what must have been in his youth a painful shyness has become in adulthood a powerful tool, to be nurtured more than it is fought off, one of the reasons he became a writer in the first place.

Influenced by Thomas Pynchon and William Gaddis, among others, DeLillo in his early books showed himself to be a writer of predominantly post-modern sensibilities; his work leaned toward the angular and ironic depiction of character and place that are associated with writers who intend to be difficult, writers who orient their fiction around its own linguistic and structural imperatives. DeLillo has spoken of creating a work that is difficult because this is one way to show, in an age of easy information, that the real truth is hard to come by. "I've always liked being relatively obscure," he says. "I feel that's where I belong, that's where my work belongs."

In many ways, the obscurity was undeserved. Unlike the writers who have influenced him, DeLillo writes with a vernacular lyricism that is never inaccessible. Unlike them as well, he produces a novel, on average, every couple of years: *Mao II* is his 10th in 20 years. His subjects—a television network programmer who hits the road in search of the big picture (*Americana*, 1971), a college football player with a nose for the apocalypse (*End Zone*, 1972), a rock star who walks off the tour (*Great Jones Street*, 1973) a teen-age mathematical genius (*Ratner's Star*, 1976), Wall Street brokers who get mixed up in a terrorist plot (*Players*, 1977), intelligence agents fighting over a rumored porno film from the *Führerbunker* (*Running Dog*, 1978), a risk analyst who crosses paths with a cult of assassins in the Middle East (*The Names*, 1982) and a professor of Hitler studies who is poisoned in an airborne toxic event (*White Noise*, 1985)—aren't exactly everyday characters. But DeLillo has brought them uncomfortably close. Here are people we know but didn't know we knew, intimate and recognizable characters on the American landscape, silhouetted figures dominated by a sense of invisibility, paranoia and dread. In many respects they are like us, except they live with an unsettling awareness of a world we prefer to ignore.

Libra (1988), DeLillo's ninth novel and his only best seller, was a fictional portrayal of Lee Harvey Oswald and the events surrounding the Kennedy assassination. "I don't think my books could have been written in the world that existed before the Kennedy assassination," DeLillo says. "And I think that some of the darkness in my work is a direct result of the confusion and psychic chaos and the sense of randomness that ensued from that moment in Dallas. It's conceivable that this made me the writer I am—for better or for worse."

DeLillo has also written two plays. *The Engineer of Moonlight*, which he wrote in the mid 1970's but never had produced, is a dazzling and mysterious piece featuring a similar set of characters to those in his new novel. *The Day Room*, about an acting troupe performing a play set in an asylum, was produced in 1986 at the American Repertory Theater in Cambridge, Mass., and in 1987 at the Manhattan Theater Club in New York.

I don't get around to asking DeLillo any biographical questions until our second meeting (same joint, same table—the comfort of familiar repetitions). Anyone who knows anything about DeLillo knows he has no interest in delving into such matters; his work is without even a trace of the usual autobiographical resonances, and the public record he has allowed to be created about his private life is minimal. When I do ask, his sentences pare down to the short and strictly declarative.

"I was born on Nov. 20, 1936," he begins, leaning an inch or two forward, toward the tape recorder. He sticks to the essential facts. Except for a short stint in Pennsylvania when he was quite young, he was brought up in the Fordham section of the Bronx, a neighborhood mostly of Italian-Americans. He lived near Arthur Avenue, with its popular food shops and restaurants. It was a childhood of sports, family and games. He played "every conceivable form of baseball," basketball and football. "No one had a football around there," he says. "We used to wrap up a bunch of newspaper with tape and use that. That was our football."

He attended Cardinal Hayes High School ("I slept for four years there") and later Fordham College, where, he says: "I didn't study much of anything. I majored in something called communication arts." The year after graduated, he got a job in advertising, as a copywriter, because he couldn't get one in publishing. He quit the job after five years or so and "embarked on my life, my real life."

I ask him what attracted him to writing, whether he studied literature or was stirred by certain authors or books. "No, no," he says, "I didn't do anything. I don't have an explanation, I don't know why I wanted to write. I did some short stories at that time, but very infrequently. I quit my job just to quit. I didn't quit my job to write fiction. I just didn't want to work anymore.

I think more than writers, the major influences on me have been European movies, and jazz, and Abstract Expressionism."

Gerald Howard, DeLillo's editor for *Libra* at Viking and now an editor at W. W. Norton, feels his own background—boyhood in an ethnic New York world, Roman Catholic schools, above-average intelligence and an interest in literature—is similar enough to DeLillo's to give him some insight into the private man. "The way I've explained Don's psychology to myself is that here is an absolutely normal guy of the sort that's very familiar to me, attached to a literary genius. And I don't think the two parts neccessarily communicate all that much."

Like *Libra*, *Mao II* appropriates certain known facts and legends. It concerns an extremely famous, obsessively reclusive author, a Salinger-Pynchon type, named Bill Gray, who eventually leaves his hermitage and enters the world of political violence. "I called him Bill Gray just as a provisional name," DeLillo says. "I used to say to friends, 'I want to change my name to Bill Gray and disappear.' I've been saying it for 10 years. But he began to fit himself into the name, and I decided to leave it."

Living with Gray in his house deep in the countryside are Scott, Gray's weird factotum and alter ego, and Scott's girlfriend, Karen, a former disciple of the Rev. Sun Myung Moon who has kind of drifted onto the scene and stuck. There is also Brita, a photographer who shoots only writers. Bill Gray beckons her to his hideout to take his picture, an uncharacteristic exposure that leads him away from his imprisoning mythology of isolation and toward a confrontation with his own death.

DeLillo gave a reading last November in New York at the 92d Street Y, in which he presented the opening passage of *Mao II* with sections from the end of *Libra*, making an interesting if subtle structural connection between them. The *Libra* passage is a monologue of half-demented, half-visionary poetry, delivered by Oswald's mother, which DeLillo based, in part, on her testimony before the Warren Commission. The section from *Mao II* is a prologue, almost the first thing DeLillo wrote when embarking on the book; it depicts a mass wedding at Yankee Stadium, performed by Moon, of 13,000 men and women, one of whom is Karen. Her parents are in the stands, with binoculars, searching for their daughter in the sea of indistinguishable faces across the outfield: "There is a strangeness down there tnat he [Karen's father] never thought he'd see in a ballpark. They take a time-honored event and repeat it, repeat it, repeat it until something new enters the world."

The Yankee Stadium prologue is an extaordinary leap of the imagination, into a scene both new and familiar, the psychic experience of the individual unburdened of selfhood and absorbed by the group, speaking and seeing with the single voice and eye of collective consciousness. The couples stand, thousands deep in the outfield, and watch their master above them: "He wears a white silk robe and a high crown figured with stylized irises. They know him at molecular level. He lives in them like chains of matter that determine who they are. This is a man of chunky build who saw Jesus on a mountainside. . . . The coupled know there are things he must leave unsaid, words whose planetary impact no one could bear. . . . This is a man who lived in a hut made of U.S. Army ration tins and now he is here, in American light, come to lead them to the end of human history."

The prologue ends, and the novel proper begins, with a passage that, in DeLillo's low-pitched and sibilant delivery, stays in the ear like words heard in a dream: "The thousands stand and chant. Around them in the world, people ride escalators going up and sneak secret glances at the faces coming down. People dangle tea bags over hot water in white cups. Cars run silently on the autobahns, streaks of painted light. People sit at desks and stare at office walls. They smell their shirts and drop them in the hamper. People bind themselves into numbered seats and fly across time zones and high cirrus and deep night, knowing there is something they've forgotten to do.

"The future belongs to crowds."

Images, especially photographs, with their insinuating, organizational power, form a narrative line in *Mao II*; they are also a part of its inspiration. "Long before he had written anything," says Nan Graham, his present editor at Viking, "Don told me he had two folders—one marked 'art' and the other marked 'terror.' "

Eventually the two folders became one. "I saw a photograph of a wedding conducted by Reverend Moon of the Unification Church," DeLillo says, "and it was just lying around for months . . . a wedding in Seoul in a soft-drink warehouse, about 13,000 people. And when I looked at it again, I realized I wanted to understand this event, and the only way to understand it was to write about it. For me, writing is a concentrated form of thinking.

"And I had another photograph—it was a picture that appeared on the front page of The New York Post, in the summer, I think, of 1988, and it was a photograph of J. D. Salinger. They sent two photographers to New Hampshire, to stalk him. It took them six days, but they found him. And they took his picture. He saw them and they saw him. When they took his picture he came at them. His face is an emblem of shock and rage. It's a frightening photograph. I didn't know it at the time, but these two pictures would represent the polar extremes of *Mao II*, the arch individualist and the mass mind, from the mind of the terrorist to the mind of the mass organization. In both cases, it's the death of the individual that has to be accomplished before their aims can be realized."

Mao II (the title comes from an Andy Warhol pencil drawing that appears briefly in the story) orients itself around certain other contemporary scenes, other photos from the art and terror folders: the ramshackle city of homeless living in Tompkins Square Park in New York, the Sheffield, England, soccer tragedy, the frenzied mourners in Teheran following the death of the Ayatollah Khomeini, the massacre at Tiananmen Square. These events come into the novel via Karen, who sees most of them on television; they form a coherent narrative of images within the larger story, images in which the individual has been crushed by the primitive and lethal instincts of mob culture. Like all of DeLillo's work, *Mao II* deals forcibly and uncannily with the ionic fears of the moment—trampling crowds, psychic unraveling, organized terror and, as always with DeLillo, isolation and death. As always too, despite how grim those descriptions may sound, there is a barbed wit, a laugh-out-loud comic grid through which his darker concerns must move.

DeLillo's early religious life, his upbringing as a Roman Catholic, has had a tangible though indirect effect on his work; a number of his characters yearn for the horror and invigoration of ancient religious spectacle. Brita, the photographer in *Mao II*, is such a character. As DeLillo says: "She needs to know that people out there believe in all the old verities, the old gods. These things keep the planet warm. But she herself is not a believer. I think there is a sense of last things in my work that probably comes from a Catholic childhood. For a Catholic, nothing is too important to discuss or think about, because he's raised with the idea that he will die any minute now and that if he doesn't live his life in a certain way this death is simply an introduction to an eternity of pain. This removes a hesitation that a writer might otherwise feel when he's approaching important subjects, eternal subjects. I think for a Catholic these things are part of ordinary life."

The rest of DeLillo's sketchy biography, to employ a phrase he uses to describe a recurring situation of his fiction, is the story of a man in small rooms. Until he was married—in 1975, to Barbara Bennett, then a banker and now a landscape designer—DeLillo lived in a studio apartment in the Murray Hill section of New York. "A small apartment with no stove and a refrigerator in the bathroom," as he put it to LeClair. (In other words, as Gerald Howard told me, and as a few others also said, "DeLillo's a monk.") Relying on savings and the intermittent income of freelance copywriting assignments, he began his first novel, *Americana*. It took him about four years to finish, and the first publisher he sent it to, Houghton Mifflin, brought it out in 1971.

There is a sense, which DeLillo talks about, that he has lived his life inside his books. During our discussion, when the first side of my tape runs out and I turn it over and begin the second, he asks me, with a sly look, "Are you sure it's working?" I immediately begin fiddling with the machine, trying to assure myself it is. "You're making me paranoid," I say, perhaps the most appropriate statement one can make to DeLillo.

"Ah, you're in the world of *White Noise* now," he says cheerfully. "There's a connection between the advances that are made in technology and the sense of primitive fear people develop in response to it. In the face of technology everything becomes a little . . . atavistic."

DeLillo equates writing with "living and breathing"; he calls working on his novels "a life and death struggle." He talks about his pleasure in "the construction of sentences and the juxtaposition of words—not just how they sound or what they mean, but even what they look like." He works on a manual typewriter, which lends to writing an almost sculptural feeling of pressing new words into blank paper. Mastering sentences, DeLillo intimates, produces its own kind of self-knowledge. Bill Gray in *Mao II* says at one point: "I'm a sentence maker. Like a donut maker, only slower." Elsewhere, he declares: "Every sentence has a truth waiting at the end of it and the writer learns how to know it when he finally gets there. On one level this truth is the swing of the sentence, the beat and poise, but down deeper it's the integrity of the writer as he matches with the language. I've always seen myself in sentences. I begin to recognize myself, word by word, as I work through a sentence. The language of my books has shaped me as a man. There's a moral force in a sentence when it comes out right. It speaks the writer's will to live."

This is one of the rare moments, it is safe to guess, when DeLillo is writing about himself.

DeLillo's books are not friendly; they don't "flatter the reader's prejudices," as Howard puts it. But if there is any comfort to be found in them, it is in that "moral force" of sentences coming out right. The architecture of DeLillo's fiction—its formal harmonies, parallel devices and symmetries and the machine-tooled precision and conviction of its language—brings an odd pleasure no matter how unsettling the world it illumines. Everyone to whom I spoke about DeLillo noted this effect. Frank Lentricchia, a prominent critic and English professor at Duke University, has written about DeLillo and taught his novels in courses. He is the editor of a recent collection of essays about the author's work called *Introducing Don DeLillo*. DeLillo's writing, he says, "represents a rare achievement in American literature—the perfect weave of novelistic imagination and cultural criticism."

Lentricchia speaks of the frustration that readers will feel if they are looking for an easily discernable moral center in DeLillo's work. "DeLillo is conducting cultural anatomies of what makes us unhappy," he says. At the same time, "the anatomist himself is full of love of language and sentences and words. There is real brio in the ways he depicts different voices and in his wit. The books have a kind of literary joy that is countervailed by the vision—so that the final prospect is both terrifying and beautiful."

The novelist and editor Gordon Lish is possibly DeLillo's closest friend—*Mao II* is dedicated to him. I ask him about a kind of emotional coldness one feels in certain of DeLillo characters, a chilliness of effect that alienates some readers. "DeLillo is a tough guy," he says. "He has no patience for what doesn't apply. It is cold, but it is a coldness one delights in. It's part of what gives you the *frisson* you are reading for in DeLillo. That chilling knowing becomes a comfort in itself. One is warmed by the absolute correctness of it. In this respect he is our most visionary writer."

The idea of a dangerous fiction, which one might bring to an analysis of DeLillo's novels, has in *Mao II* become an expressed element of his plot. Bill Gray sees the novelist as both dangerous and threatened. Charles Everson, Gray's former editor, tells him: "You have a twisted sense of the writer's place in society. You think the writer belongs at the far margin, doing dangerous things. In Central America, writers carry guns. They have to. And this has always been your idea of the way it ought to be. The state should want to kill all writers. Every government, every group that holds power or aspires to power should feel so threatened by writers that they hunt them down, everywhere."

Says Gerald Howard: "On the grubby commercial level, there is going to be a lot of buzz about Bill Gray and who he's meant to be, what parts of him have been taken from Pynchon and Salinger and so on. But I think this is a book that's about Salman Rushdie in a way. Don was very upset about the Rushdie business, and I think that you can sense that feeling of threat all the way through *Mao II*."

In fact, DeLillo was one of the authors who read at the Columns in New York City, an occasion of support for Rushdie organized by the Authors' Guild, PEN American Center and Article 19. The reading, which took place under heavy security, has a close parallel in *Mao II*. The big difference is that, in the book, the violence that everyone is afraid of actually occurs.

Interestingly, Nan Graham is also Rushdie's American editor, and Rushdie, like DeLillo, also worked as an advertising copywriter for the same firm DeLillo worked for, Ogilvy & Mather. I ask DeLillo about the connection of the book to Rushdie's situation. "I don't know how deep it is," he says, "but it's there. It's the connection between the writer as the champion of the self, and those forces that are threatened by this. Such totalitarian movements can be seen in miniature in the very kind of situation Rushdie is in. He's a hostage."

The threat to the writer comes in the dramatic form of violence, but it is also present in its more mundane disguises. There's a passage in the book where Bill Gray grumbles about the publishing industry, its quick fashions and hot new excitements. "The more books they publish, the weaker we become," he says. "The secret force that drives the industry is the compulsion to make writers harmless."

"I don't know if I agree with him," DeLillo remarks. "But I do think we can connect novelists and terrorists here. In a repressive society, a writer can be deeply influential, but in a society that's filled with glut and repetition and endless consumption, the act of terror may be the only meaningful act. People who are in power make their arrangements in secret, largely as a way of maintaining and furthering that power. People who are powerless make an open theater of violence. True terror is a language and a vision. There is a deep narrative structure to terrorist acts, and they infiltrate and alter con-sciousness in ways that writers used to aspire to."

The implication is that, should writers aspire to do so again, they too will be among the nationless, the outcast and the hunted. DeLillo tells the story of a friend of his, living in Athens: "Somebody fired a shot through his window recently. And this guy is writing fiction for the first time in his life. He's in his forties; he's writing a novel. Of course, he told the police that he assumed the

shot had been fired at him because he's an American. And so I wrote him a
note and I said, 'They're not shooting at you because you're an American,
they're shooting at you because you're a novelist.'"

And then he laughs. It is a moment of mischievous pleasure in the darker
workings of his imagination: bombs making blossoms of plate-glass windows,
bullets pocking the plasterwork. Nasty images, certainly, but images of the
day—and terrifying evidence of the real power of art.

The Art of Fiction CXXXV: Don DeLillo

Adam Begley / 1993

From *The Paris Review* # 128, Fall 1993, pp. 274–306. Reprinted by permission of *The Paris Review*. Copyright © 1993 *The Paris Review*.

A man who's been called "the chief shaman of the paranoid school of American fiction" can be expected to act a little nervous.

I met Don DeLillo for the first time in an Irish restaurant in Manhattan, for a conversation he said would be "deeply preliminary." He is a slender man, gray haired, with boxy brown glasses. His eyes, magnified by thick lenses, are restless without being shifty. He looks to the right, to the left; he turns his head to see what's behind him.

But his edgy manner has nothing to do with anxiety. He's a disciplined observer searching for details. I also discovered after many hours of interviewing spread out over several days—a quick lunch, a visit some months later to a midtown gallery to see an Anselm Kiefer installation, followed by a drink at a comically posh bar—that DeLillo is a kind man, generous and thoughtful, qualities incompatible with the reflexive wariness of the paranoid. He is not scared; he is attentive. His smile is shy, his laugh sudden.

Don DeLillo's parents came to America from Italy. He was born in the Bronx in 1936 and grew up there, in an Italian-American neighborhood. He attended Cardinal Hayes High School and Fordham University, where he majored in "communication arts," and worked for a time as a copywriter at Ogilvy & Mather, an advertising agency. He now lives just outside New York City with his wife.

Americana, his first novel, was published in 1971. It took him about four years to write. At the time he was living in a small studio apartment in Manhattan. After Americana *the novels poured out in a rush: five more in the next seven years.* End Zone *(1972),* Great Jones Street *(1973),* Ratner's Star *(1976),* Players *(1977) and* Running Dog *(1978) all received enthusiastic reviews. They did not sell well. The books were known to a small but loyal following.*

Things changed in the eighties. The Names *(1982) was more prominently reviewed than any previous DeLillo novel.* White Noise *(1985) won the*

National Book Award. Libra *(1988) was a bestseller.* Mao II, *his latest, won the* 1992 PEN/Faulkner Award. *He is currently at work on a novel, a portion of which appeared in* Harper's *under the title "Pafko at the Wall." He has written two plays,* The Engineer of Moonlight *(1979) and* The Day Room *(1986).*

This interview began in the fall of 1992 as a series of tape-recorded conversations. Transcripts were made from eight hours of taped material. DeLillo returned the final, edited manuscript with a note that begins, "This is not only the meat but the potatos."

Interviewer: Do you have any idea what made you a writer?
DeLillo: I have an idea but I'm not sure I believe it. Maybe I wanted to learn how to think. Writing is a concentrated form of thinking. I don't know what I think about certain subjects, even today, until I sit down and try to write about them. Maybe I wanted to find more rigorous ways of thinking. We're talking now about the earliest writing I did and about the power of language to counteract the wallow of late adolescence, to define things, define muddled experience in economical ways. Let's not forget that writing is convenient. It requires the simplest tools. A young writer sees that with words and sentences on a piece of paper that costs less than a penny he can place himself more clearly in the world. Words on a page, that's all it takes to help him separate himself from the forces around him, streets and people and pressures and feelings. He learns to think about these things, to ride his own sentences into new perceptions. How much of this did I feel at the time? Maybe just an inkling, an instinct. Writing was mainly an unnameable urge, an urge partly propelled by the writers I was reading at the time.

Interviewer: Did you read as a child?
DeLillo: No, not at all. Comic books. This is probably why I don't have a storytelling drive, a drive to follow a certain kind of narrative rhythm.

Interviewer: As a teenager?
DeLillo: Not much at first. *Dracula* when I was fourteen. A spider eats a fly, and a rat eats the spider, and a cat eats the rat, and a dog eats the cat, and maybe somebody eats the dog. Did I miss one level of devouring? And yes, the *Studs Lonigan* trilogy, which showed me that my own life, or something like it, could be the subject of a writer's scrutiny. This was an amazing thing to discover. Then, when I was eighteen, I got a summer job as a playground

attendant—a parkie. And I was told to wear a white T-shirt and brown pants and brown shoes and a whistle around my neck—which they provided, the whistle. But I never acquired the rest of the outfit. I wore blue jeans and checkered shirts and kept the whistle in my pocket and just sat on a park bench disguised as an ordinary citizen. And this is where I read Faulkner, *As I Lay Dying* and *Light in August*. And got paid for it. And then James Joyce, and it was through Joyce that I learned to see something in language that carried a radiance, something that made me feel the beauty and fervor of words, the sense that a word has a life and a history. And I'd look at a sentence in *Ulysses* or in *Moby-Dick* or in Hemingway—maybe I hadn't gotten to *Ulysses* at that point, it was *Portrait of the Artist*—but certainly Hemingway and the water that was clear and swiftly moving and the way the troops went marching down the road and raised dust that powdered the leaves of the trees. All this in a playground in the Bronx.

Interviewer: Does the fact that you grew up in an Italian-American household translate in some way, does it show up in the novels you've published?
DeLillo: It showed up in early short stories. I think it translates to the novels only in the sense that it gave me a perspective from which to see the larger environment. It's no accident that my first novel was called *Americana*. This was a private declaration of independence, a statement of my intention to use the whole picture, the whole culture. America was and is the immigrant's dream, and as the son of two immigrants I was attracted by the sense of possibility that had drawn my grandparents and parents. This was a subject that would allow me to develop a range I hadn't shown in those early stories—a range and a freedom. And I was well into my twenties by this point and had long since left the streets where I'd grown up. Not left them forever—I do want to write about those years. It's just a question of finding the right frame.

Interviewer: What got you started on *Americana*?
DeLillo: I don't always know when or where an idea first hits the nervous system, but I remember *Americana*. I was sailing in Maine with two friends, and we put into a small harbor on Mt. Desert Island. And I was sitting on a railroad tie waiting to take a shower, and I had a glimpse of a street maybe fifty yards away and a sense of beautiful old houses and rows of elms and maples and a stillness and wistfulness—the street seemed to carry its own built-in longing. And I felt something, a pause, something opening up

before me. It would be a month or two before I started writing the book and two or three years before I came up with the title *Americana*, but in fact it was all implicit in that moment—a moment in which nothing happened, nothing ostensibly changed, a moment in which I didn't see anything I hadn't seen before. But there was a pause in time, and I knew I had to write about a man who comes to a street like this or lives on a street like this. And whatever roads the novel eventually followed, I believe I maintained the idea of that quiet street if only as counterpoint, as lost innocence.

Interviewer: Do you think it made a difference in your career that you started writing novels late, when you were approaching thirty?
DeLillo: Well, I wish I had started earlier, but evidently I wasn't ready. First, I lacked ambition. I may have had novels in my head but very little on paper and no personal goals, no burning desire to achieve some end. Second, I didn't have a sense of what it takes to be a serious writer. It took me a long time to develop this. Even when I was well into my first novel I didn't have a system for working, a dependable routine. I worked haphazardly, sometimes late at night, sometimes in the afternoon. I spent too much time doing other things or nothing at all. On humid summer nights I tracked horseflies through the apartment and killed them—not for the meat but because they were driving me crazy with their buzzing. I hadn't developed a sense of the level of dedication that's necessary to do this kind of work.

Interviewer: What are your working habits now?
DeLillo: I work in the morning at a manual typewriter. I do about four hours and then go running. This helps me shake off one world and enter another. Trees, birds, drizzle—it's a nice kind of interlude. Then I work again, later afternoon, for two or three hours. Back into book time, which is transparent—you don't know it's passing. No snack food or coffee. No cigarettes—I stopped smoking a long time ago. The space is clear, the house is quiet. A writer takes earnest measures to secure his solitude and then finds endless ways to squander it. Looking out the window, reading random entries in the dictionary. To break the spell I look at a photograph of Borges, a great picture sent to me by the Irish writer Colm Tóibín. The face of Borges against a dark background—Borges fierce, blind, his nostrils gaping, his skin stretched taut, his mouth amazingly vivid; his mouth looks painted; he's like a shaman painted for visions, and the whole face has a kind of steely rapture. I've read

Borges of course, although not nearly all of it, and I don't know anything about the way he worked—but the photograph shows us a writer who did not waste time at the window or anywhere else. So I've tried to make him my guide out of lethargy and drift, into the otherworld of magic, art and divination.

Interviewer: Do your typed drafts just pile up and sit around?
DeLillo: That's right. I want those pages nearby because there's always a chance I'll have to refer to something that's scrawled at the bottom of a sheet of paper somewhere. Discarded pages mark the physical dimensions of a writer's labor—you know, how many shots it took to get a certain paragraph right. Or the awesome accumulation, the gross tonnage, of first draft pages. The first draft of *Libra* sits in ten manuscript boxes. I like knowing it's in the house. I feel connected to it. It's the complete book, the full experience containable on paper. I find I'm more ready to discard pages than I used to be. I used to look for things to keep. I used to find ways to save a paragraph or a sentence, maybe by relocating it. Now I look for ways to discard things. If I discard a sentence I like, it's almost as satisfying as keeping a sentence I like. I don't think I've become ruthless or perverse—just a bit more willing to believe that nature will restore itself. The instinct to discard is finally a kind of faith. It tells me there's a better way to do this page even though the evidence is not accessible at the present time.

Interviewer: Athletes—basketball players, football players—talk about "getting into the zone." Is there a writer's zone you get into?
DeLillo: There's a zone I aspire to. Finding it is another question. It's a state of automatic writing, and it represents the paradox that's at the center of a writer's consciousness—this writer's anyway. First you look for discipline and control. You want to exercise your will, bend the language your way, bend the world your way. You want to control the flow of impulses, images, words, faces, ideas. But there's a higher place, a secret aspiration. You want to let go. You want to lose yourself in language, become a carrier or messenger. The best moments involve a loss of control. It's a kind of rapture, and it can happen with words and phrases fairly often—completely surprising combinations that make a higher kind of sense, that come to you out of nowhere. But rarely for extended periods, for paragraphs and pages—I think poets must have more access to this state than novelists do. In *End Zone* a number of

characters play a game of touch football in a snowstorm. There's nothing rapturous or magical about the writing. The writing is simple. But I wrote the passage, maybe five or six pages, in a state of pure momentum, without the slightest pause or deliberation.

Interviewer: How do you imagine your audience?
DeLillo: When my head is in the typewriter the last thing on my mind is some imaginary reader. I don't have an audience; I have a set of standards. But when I think of my work out in the world, written and published, I like to imagine it's being read by some stranger somewhere who doesn't have anyone around him to talk to about books and writing—maybe a would-be writer, maybe a little lonely, who depends on a certain kind of writing to make him feel more comfortable in the world.

Interviewer: I've read critics who say that your books are bound to make people feel uncomfortable.
DeLillo: Well, that's good to know. But this reader we're talking about—he already feels uncomfortable. He's very uncomfortable. And maybe what he needs is a book that will help him realize he's not alone.

Interviewer: How do you begin? What are the raw materials of a story?
DeLillo: I think the scene comes first, an idea of a character in a place. It's visual, it's Technicolor—something I see in a vague way. Then sentence by sentence into the breach. No outlines—maybe a short list of items, chronological, that may represent the next twenty pages. But the basic work is built around the sentence. This is what I mean when I call myself a writer. I construct sentences. There's a rhythm I hear that drives me through a sentence. And the words typed on the white page have a sculptural quality. They form odd correspondences. They match up not just through meaning but through sound and look. The rhythm of a sentence will accommodate a certain number of syllables. One syllable too many, I look for another word. There's always another word that means nearly the same thing, and if it doesn't then I'll consider altering the meaning of a sentence to keep the rhythm, the syllable beat. I'm completely willing to let language press meaning upon me. Watching the way in which words match up, keeping the balance in a sentence—these are sensuous pleasures. I might want *very* and *only* in the same sentence, spaced a particular way, exactly so far apart. I might want

rapture matched with *danger*—I like to match word endings. I type rather
than write longhand because I like the way the words and letters look when
they come off the hammers onto the page—finished, printed, beautifully
formed.

Interviewer: Do you care about paragraphs?

DeLillo: When I was working on *The Names* I devised a new method—new
to me, anyway. When I finished a paragraph, even a three-line paragraph, I
automatically went to a fresh page to start the new paragraph. No crowded
pages. This enabled me to see a given set of sentences more clearly. It made
rewriting easier and more effective. The white space on the page helped me
concentrate more deeply on what I'd written. And with this book I tried to
find a deeper level of seriousness as well. *The Names* is the book that marks
the beginning of a new dedication. I needed the invigoration of unfamiliar
languages and new landscapes, and I worked to find a clarity of prose that
might serve as an equivalent to the clear light of those Aegean islands. The
Greeks made an art of the alphabet, a visual art, and I studied the shapes of
letters carved on stones all over Athens. This gave me fresh energy and forced
me to think more deeply about what I was putting on the page. Some of the
work I did in the 1970s was off-the-cuff, not powerfully motivated. I think
I forced my way into a couple of books that weren't begging to be written, or
maybe I was writing too fast. Since then I've tried to be patient, to wait for a
subject to take me over, become part of my life beyond the desk and typewriter. *Libra* was a great experience that continues to resonate in my mind
because of the fascinating and tragic lives that were part of the story. And
The Names keeps resonating because of the languages I heard and read and
touched and tried to speak and spoke a little and because of the sunlight
and the elemental landscapes that I tried to blend into the book's sentences
and paragraphs.

Interviewer: Your dialogue is different from other people's dialogue.

DeLillo: Well, there are fifty-two ways to write dialogue that's faithful to the
way people speak. And then there are times when you're not trying to be
faithful. I've done it different ways myself and I think I concentrated on dialogue most deeply in *Players*. It's hyperrealistic, spoken by urban men and
women who live together, who know each other's speech patterns and
thought patterns and finish each other's sentences or don't even bother

because it isn't necessary. Jumpy, edgy, a bit hostile, dialogue that's almost obsessive about being funny whatever the circumstances. New York voices.

Interviewer: Has the way you handle dialogue evolved?
DeLillo: It has evolved, but maybe sideways. I don't have a grand, unified theory. I think about dialogue differently from book to book. In *The Names* I raised the level of intelligence and perception. People speak a kind of idealized café dialogue. In *Libra* I flattened things out. The characters are bigger and broader, the dialogue is flatter. There were times with Oswald, with his marine buddies and with his wife and mother when I used a documentary approach. They speak the flat prose of *The Warren Report*.

Interviewer: You mentioned early short stories. Do you ever write stories anymore?
DeLillo: Fewer all the time.

Interviewer: Could the set piece—I'm thinking of the Unification Church wedding in *Mao II* or the in-flight movie in *Players*—be your alternative to the short story?
DeLillo: I don't think of them that way. What attracts me to this format is its non-short-storyness, the high degree of stylization. In *Players* all the major characters in the novel appear in the prologue—embryonically, not yet named or defined. They're shadowy people watching a movie on an airplane. This piece is the novel in miniature. It lies outside the novel. It's modular— keep it in or take it out. The mass wedding in *Mao II* is more conventional. It introduces a single major character and sets up themes and resonances. The book makes no sense without it.

Interviewer: We talked a little about *Americana*. Tell me about your second novel—what was your idea for the shape of *End Zone*?
DeLillo: I don't think I had an idea. I had a setting and some characters, and I more or less trailed behind, listening. At some point I realized there had to be a structural core, and I decided to play a football game. This became the centerpiece of the novel. The same thing happens in *White Noise*. There's an aimless shuffle toward a high-intensity event—this time a toxic spill that forces people to evacuate their homes. Then, in each book, there's a kind of decline, a purposeful loss of energy. Otherwise I think the two books are

quite different. *End Zone* is about games—war, language, football. In *White Noise* there is less language and more human dread. There's a certain equation at work. As technology advances in complexity and scope, fear becomes more primitive.

Interviewer: Plot, in the shape of shadowy conspiracy, shows up for the first time in your third novel, *Great Jones Street*. What brought you to write about the idea of a mysterious drug possibly tied to government repression?
DeLillo: It was in the air. It was the way people were thinking. Those were the days when the enemy was some presence seeping out of the government, and the most paranoid sort of fear was indistinguishable from common sense. I think I tried to get at the slickness connected with the word *paranoia*. It was becoming a kind of commodity. It used to mean one thing and after a while it began to mean everything. It became something you bought into, like Club Med.

Interviewer: Were you looking for a plot?
DeLillo: I think the plot found me. In a book about fear and paranoia, a plot was bound to assert itself. It's not the tightest sort of plotting—more like drug fantasies, seeing dead relatives come out of the walls. What we finally have is a man in a small room, a man who has shut himself away, and this is something that happens in my work—the man hiding from acts of violence or planning acts of violence, or the individual reduced to silence by the forces around him.

Interviewer: The most lyrical language in *Great Jones Street* is reserved for the last chapter. Bucky Wunderlick, deprived of the faculty of speech, is wandering the streets of lower Manhattan. Why did you apply such poetic beauty to these scenes of dereliction?
DeLillo: I think this is how urban people react to the deteriorating situation around them—I think we need to invent beauty, search out some restoring force. A writer may describe the ugliness and pain in graphic terms but he can also try to find a dignity and significance in ruined parts of the city, and the people he sees there. Ugly and beautiful—this is part of the tension of *Great Jones Street*. When I was working on the book there were beggars and derelicts in parts of the city they'd never entered before. A sense of failed souls and forgotten lives on a new scale. And the place began to feel a little

like a community in the Middle Ages. Disease on the streets, insane people talking to themselves, the drug culture spreading among the young. We're talking about the very early 1970s, and I remember thinking of New York as a European city in the fourteenth century. Maybe this is why I was looking for a ruined sort of grandeur in the language at the end of the book.

Interviewer: There's a three-year period between *Great Jones Street* and your next book, *Ratner's Star*. Did it take you all that time to write it?
DeLillo: It took a little over two years of extremely concentrated work. I'm amazed now that I was able to do the book in that period of time. I was drawn to the beauty of scientific language, the mystery of numbers, the idea of pure mathematics as a secret history and secret language—and to the notion of a fourteen-year-old mathematical genius at the center of all this. I guess it's also a book of games, mathematics being chief among them. It's a book in which structure predominates. The walls, the armature, the foundation—I wandered inside this thing I was building and sometimes felt taken over by it, not so much lost inside it as helpless to prevent the thing from building new connections, new underground links.

Interviewer: What got you so interested in mathematics?
DeLillo: Mathematics is underground knowledge. Only the actual practitioners know the terms and references. And I was drawn to the idea of a novel about an enormously important field of human thought that remains largely unknown. But I had to enter as a novice, a jokesmith, with a certain sly deference. I had to sneak up on my subject. No other book I've done was at the same time such fun and such labor. And all the time I was writing the book I was writing a shadow book in another part of my mind—same story, same main character but a small book, a book the size of a children's book, maybe it *was* a children's book, less structure, less weight—four characters instead of eighty-four or a hundred and four.

Interviewer: What you actually wrote is very different from your first three books.
DeLillo: Somebody said that *Ratner's Star* is the monster at the center of my work. But maybe it's in orbit around the other books. I think the other books

constitute a single compact unit and that *Ratner's Star* swings in orbit around this unit at a very great distance.

Interviewer: Your next book was *Players*.

DeLillo: Structure again but in a completely different way. Structure as something people need in their lives. It's about double lives. The second life is not only the secret life. It's the more structured life. People need rules and boundaries, and if society doesn't provide them in sufficient measure, the estranged individual may drift into something deeper and more dangerous. Terrorism is built on structure. A terrorist act is a structured narrative played out over days or weeks or even years if there are hostages involved. What we call the shadow life of terrorists or gun runners or double agents is in fact the place where a certain clarity takes effect, where definitions matter, and both sides tend to follow the same set of rules.

Interviewer: Owen Brademas, a character in *The Names*, makes some interesting remarks about the novel. At one point he says, "If I were a writer, how would I enjoy being told the novel is dead. How liberating to work in the margins outside the central perception. You are the ghoul of literature."

DeLillo: The novel's not dead, it's not even seriously injured, but I do think we're working in the margins, working in the shadows of the novel's greatness and influence. There's plenty of impressive talent around, and there's strong evidence that younger writers are moving into history, finding broader themes. But when we talk about the novel we have to consider the culture in which it operates. Everything in the culture argues against the novel, particularly the novel that tries to be equal to the complexities and excesses of the culture. This is why books such as *JR* and *Harlot's Ghost* and *Gravity's Rainbow* and *The Public Burning* are important—to name just four. They offer many pleasures without making concessions to the middle-range reader, and they absorb and incorporate the culture instead of catering to it. And there's the work of Robert Stone and Joan Didion, who are both writers of conscience and painstaking workers of the sentence and paragraph. I don't want to list names because lists are a form of cultural hysteria, but I have to mention *Blood Meridian* for its beauty and its honor. These books and writers show us that the novel is still spacious enough and brave enough to encompass enormous areas of experience. We have a rich literature. But sometimes it's a literature too ready to be neutralized, to be incorporated into the ambient noise. This is why we need the writer in opposition, the novelist who writes against power, who writes against the corporation or the state or the whole apparatus of assimilation. We're all one beat away from becoming elevator music.

Interviewer: Could you tell me about the passage in *White Noise* in which Jack listens to his daughter Steffie talking in her sleep, and she is repeating the words *Toyota Celica*?

DeLillo: There's something nearly mystical about certain words and phrases that float through our lives. It's computer mysticism. Words that are computer generated to be used on products that might be sold anywhere from Japan to Denmark—words devised to be pronounceable in a hundred languages. And when you detach one of these words from the product it was designed to serve, the word acquires a chantlike quality. Years ago somebody decided—I don't know how this conclusion was reached—that the most beautiful phrase in the English language was *cellar door*. If you concentrate on the sound, if you disassociate the words from the object they denote, and if you say the words over and over, they become a sort of higher Esperanto. This is how *Toyota Celica* began its life. It was pure chant at the beginning. Then they had to find an object to accommodate the words.

Interviewer: Tell me about the research you did for *Libra*.

DeLillo: There were several levels of research—fiction writer's research. I was looking for ghosts, not living people. I went to New Orleans, Dallas, Fort Worth and Miami and looked at houses and streets and hospitals, schools and libraries—this is mainly Oswald I'm tracking but others as well—and after a while the characters in my mind and in my notebooks came out into the world.

Then there were books, old magazines, old photographs, scientific reports, material printed by obscure presses, material my wife turned up from relatives in Texas. And a guy in Canada with a garage full of amazing stuff—audiotapes of Oswald talking on a radio program, audiotapes of his mother reading from his letters. And I looked at film consisting of amateur footage shot in Dallas on the day of the assassination, crude powerful footage that included the Zapruder film. And there were times when I felt an eerie excitement, coming across an item that seemed to bear out my own theories.

Anyone who enters this maze knows you have to become part scientist, novelist, biographer, historian and existential detective. The landscape was crawling with secrets, and this novel-in-progress was my own precious secret—I told very few people what I was doing.

Then there was *The Warren Report*, which is the *Oxford English Dictionary* of the assassination and also the Joycean novel. This is the one document that captures the full richness and madness and meaning of the event, despite the fact that it omits about a ton and a half of material. I'm not an obsessive researcher, and I think I read maybe half of *The Warren Report*, which totals twenty-six volumes. There are acres of FBI reports I barely touched. But for me the boring and meaningless stretches are part of the experience. This is what a life resembles in its starkest form—school records, lists of possessions, photographs of knotted string found in a kitchen drawer. It took seven seconds to kill the president, and we're still collecting evidence and sifting documents and finding people to talk to and working through the trivia. The trivia is exceptional. When I came across the dental records of Jack Ruby's mother I felt a surge of admiration. Did they really put this in? The testimony of witnesses was a great resource—period language, regional slang, the twisted syntax of Marguerite Oswald and others as a kind of improvised genius and the lives of trainmen and stripteasers and telephone clerks. I had to be practical about this, and so I resisted the urge to read everything.

Interviewer: When *Libra* came out, I had the feeling that this was a magnum opus, a life accomplishment. Did you know what you would do next?

DeLillo: I thought I would be haunted by this story and these characters for some time to come, and that turned out to be true. But it didn't affect the search for new material, the sense that it was time to start thinking about a new book. *Libra* will have a lingering effect on me partly because I became so deeply involved in the story and partly because the story doesn't have an end out here in the world beyond the book—new theories, new suspects and new documents keep turning up. It will never end. And there's no reason it should end. At the time of the twenty-fifth anniversary one newspaper titled its story about the assassination "The Day America Went Crazy." About the same time I became aware of three rock groups—or maybe two rock groups and a folk group—touring at the same time: the Oswalds, the Jack Rubies and the Dead Kennedys.

Interviewer: How do you normally feel at the end of writing a novel? Are you disgusted with what you've done? Pleased?

DeLillo: I'm usually happy to finish and uncertain about what I've done. This is where you have to depend on other people, editors, friends, other readers. But the strangest thing that happened to me at the end of a book concerns *Libra*. I had a photograph of Oswald propped on a makeshift bookshelf on my desk, the photo in which he holds a rifle and some left-wing journals. It was there for nearly the entire time I was working on the book, about three years and three months. When I reached the last sentence—a sentence whose precise wording I knew long before I reached the final page, a sentence I'd been eager to get to and which, when I finally got to it, I probably typed at a faster than usual rate, feeling the deepest sort of relief and satisfaction—the picture started sliding off the shelf, and I had to pause to catch it.

Interviewer: There was a passage in a critical work about you that disturbed me a bit—I don't know if it came from an interview you gave or just a supposition on the writer's part—in which it was claimed that you don't particularly care about your characters.

DeLillo: A character is part of the pleasure a writer wants to give his readers. A character who lives, who says interesting things. I want to give pleasure through language, through the architecture of a book or a sentence and through characters who may be funny, nasty, violent or all of these. But I'm not the kind of writer who dotes on certain characters and wants readers to do the same. The fact is every writer likes his characters to the degree that he's able to work out their existence. You invent a character who pushes his mother down a flight of stairs, say. She's an old lady in a wheelchair and your character comes home drunk and pushes her down a long flight of stairs. Do you automatically dislike this man? He's done an awful thing. But I don't believe it's that simple. Your feelings toward this character depend on whether or not you've realized him fully, whether you understand him. It's not a simple question of like or dislike. And you don't necessarily show your feelings toward a character in the same way you show feelings to real people. In *Mao II* I felt enormous sympathy toward Karen Janney, sympathy, understanding, kinship. I was able to enter her consciousness quickly and easily. And I tried to show this sympathy and kinship through the language I used when writing from her viewpoint—a free-flowing, non-sequitur ramble that's completely different from the other characters' view-points. Karen is not especially likable. But once I'd given her a life independent of my own will, I had no choice but to like her—although it's simplistic to put it that way—and it shows in the sentences I wrote, which are free of the usual constraints that bind words to a sentence in a certain way.

Interviewer: Did you try with *Libra* for a larger audience than you had achieved at the time of *The Names*?

DeLillo: I wouldn't know how to do that. My mind works one way, toward making a simple moment complex, and this is not the way to gain a larger audience. I think I have the audience my work ought to have. It's not easy work. And you have to understand that I started writing novels fairly late and with low expectations. I didn't even think of myself as a writer until I was two years into my first novel. When I was struggling with that book I felt unlucky, unblessed by the fates and by the future, and almost everything that has happened since then has proved me wrong. So some of my natural edginess and pessimism has been tempered by acceptance. This hasn't softened the tone of my work—it has simply made me realize I've had a lucky life as a writer.

Interviewer: I can see how *Mao II* would come naturally out of *Libra* from a thematic point of view—the terrorist and the man in the small room. But I'm curious as to why, after *Libra*, you went back to the shape and feel of your previous novels. There's something about the wandering in *Mao II* that goes back to *Players* or *Running Dog*.

DeLillo: The bare structure of *Mao II* is similar to the way *Players* is set up, including a prologue and an epilogue. But *Mao II* is a sort of rest-and-motion book, to invent a category. The first half of the book could have been called "The Book." Bill Gray talking about his book, piling up manuscript pages, living in a house that operates as a kind of filing cabinet for his work and all the other work it engenders. And the second half of the book could have been called "The World." Here, Bill escapes his book and enters the world. It turns out to be the world of political violence. I was nearly finished with the first half of the book before I realized how the second half ought to be shaped. I was writing blind. It was a struggle up to that point, but once I understood that Bill had to escape his handlers—the most obvious things tend to take the form of startling revelations—I felt a surge of excitement because the book had finally revealed itself to me.

Interviewer: We talked briefly about men in small rooms. Bill Gray the writer. Lee Oswald the plotter. Owen Brademas in the old city of Lahore. Bucky Wunderlick blown off the concert stage and hiding out. But what about the crowd? "The future belongs to crowds," you wrote in *Mao II*. That sentence gets quoted a lot.

DeLillo: In *Mao II* I thought about the secluded writer, the arch individualist, living outside the glut of the image world. And then the crowd, many kinds of crowds, people in soccer stadiums, people gathered around enormous photographs of holy men or heads of state. This book is an argument about the future. Who wins the struggle for the imagination of the world? There was a time when the inner world of the novelist—Kafka's private vision and maybe Beckett's—eventually folded into the three-dimensional world we were all living in. These men wrote a kind of world narrative. And so did Joyce in another sense. Joyce turned the book into a world with *Ulysses* and *Finnegans Wake*. Today, the world has become a book—more precisely a news story or television show or piece of film footage. And the world narrative is being written by men who orchestrate disastrous events, by military leaders, totalitarian leaders, terrorists, men dazed by power. World news is the novel people want to read. It carries the tragic narrative that used to belong to the novel. The crowds in *Mao II*, except for the mass wedding, are TV crowds, masses of people we see in news coverage of terrible events. The news has been full of crowds, and the TV audience represents another kind of crowd. The crowd broken down into millions of small rooms.

Interviewer: One of the funnier moments in *Mao II*—it's a typically grim funny moment—is when Bill Gray has been run over by a car, and he approaches a group of veterinarians to try to determine the extent of his damage. Where did that come from?

DeLillo: I said something earlier about going from simple to complex moments. This is one of those instances. I wanted to reveal the seriousness of Bill Gray's physical condition, but it seemed ridiculously simple to have him walk into a doctor's office. Partly because he didn't want to see a doctor—he feared the blunt truth—but mainly because I wanted to do something more interesting. So I took an indirect route and hoped for certain riches along the way. I wanted to make basic medical information an occasion for comic dialogue and for an interesting play of levels. What I mean is that Bill pretends to be a writer—of course, he *is* a writer—doing research on a medical matter he wants to put into his book. This happens to be exactly what I did before writing the passage. I talked to a doctor about the kind of injury Bill suffered when the car hit him and what the consequences might be and how the effects of the injury might manifest themselves. And I played his answers back through the medium of three tipsy British veterinarians trying to oblige a stranger who may actually be gravely ill and isn't sure how he feels about it. Bill the writer becomes his own character. He tries to shade the information, soften it a bit, by establishing a kind of fiction. He needs this for a book, he tells them, but it turned out to be my book, not his.

Interviewer: There are a number of characters in your work who discover that they are going to die sooner than they thought, though they don't know exactly when. Bucky Wunderlick isn't going to die, but he's been given something awful, and for all he knows the side effects are deadly; Jack Gladney, poisoned by the toxic spill, is another obvious example; and then we come to Bill Gray with his automobile accident. What does this accelerated but vague mortality mean?

DeLillo: Who knows? If writing is a concentrated form of thinking, then the most concentrated writing probably ends in some kind of reflection on dying. This is what we eventually confront if we think long enough and hard enough.

Interviewer: Could it be related to the idea in *Libra* that—

DeLillo: —all plots lead toward death? I guess that's possible. It happens in *Libra*, and it happens in *White Noise*, which doesn't necessarily mean that these are highly plotted novels. *Libra* has many digressions and meditations, and Oswald's life just meanders along for much of the book. It's the original plotter, Win Everett, who wonders if his conspiracy might grow tentacles that will turn an assassination *scare* into an actual murder, and of course this is what happens. The plot extends its own logic to the ultimate point. And *White Noise* develops a trite adultery plot that enmeshes the hero, justifying his fears about the death energies contained in plots. When I think of highly plotted novels I think of detective fiction or mystery fiction, the kind of work that always produces a few dead bodies. But these bodies are basically plot points, not worked-out characters. The book's plot either moves inexorably toward a dead body or flows directly from it, and the more artificial the situation the better. Readers can play off their fears by encountering the death experience in a superficial way. A mystery novel localizes the awesome force of the real death outside the book, winds it tightly in a plot, makes it less fearful by containing it in a kind of game format.

Interviewer: You've said that you didn't think your books could be written in the world that existed before the Kennedy assassination.
DeLillo: Our culture changed in important ways. And these changes are among the things that go into my work. There's the shattering randomness of the event, the missing motive, the violence that people not only commit but seem to watch simultaneously from a disinterested distance. Then the uncertainty we feel about the basic facts that surround the case—number of gunmen, number of shots and so on. Our grip on reality has felt a little threatened. Every revelation about the event seems to produce new levels of secrecy, unexpected links, and I guess this has been part of my work, the clandestine mentality—how ordinary people spy on themselves, how the power centers operate and manipulate. Our postwar history has seen tanks in the streets and occasional massive force. But mainly we have the individual in the small room, the nobody who walks out of the shadows and changes everything. That week in Maine, that street I saw that made me think I had to write a novel—well, I bought a newspaper the same day or maybe later in the week, and there was a story about Charles Whitman, the young man who went to the top of a tower in Austin, Texas and shot and killed over a dozen people and wounded about thirty more. Took a number of guns up there with him. Took supplies with him, ready for a long siege, including underarm deodorant. And I remember thinking, Texas again. And also, underarm deodorant. That was my week in Maine.

Interviewer: One of the other things that's very important in *Libra* is the existence of a filmed version of the assassination. One of the points you make is that television didn't really come into its own until it filmed Oswald's murder. Is it possible that one of the things that marks you as a writer is that you're a post-television writer?
DeLillo: Kennedy was shot on film, Oswald was shot on TV. Does this mean anything? Maybe only that Oswald's death became instantly repeatable. It belonged to everyone. The Zapruder film, the film of Kennedy's death, was sold and hoarded and doled out very selectively. It was exclusive footage. So that the social differences continued to pertain, the hierarchy held fast—you

could watch Oswald die while you ate a TV dinner, and he was still dying by the time you went to bed, but if you wanted to see the Zapruder film you had to be very important or you had to wait until the 1970s when I believe it was shown once on television, or you had to pay somebody thirty thousand dollars to look at it—I think that's the going rate.

The Zapruder film is a home movie that runs about eighteen seconds and could probably fuel college courses in a dozen subjects from history to physics. And every new generation of technical experts gets to take a crack at the Zapruder film. The film represents all the hopefulness we invest in technology. A new enhancement technique or a new computer analysis—not only of Zapruder but of other key footage and still photographs—will finally tell us precisely what happened.

Interviewer: I read it exactly the opposite way, which may be also what you're getting around to. It's one of the great ironies that, despite the existence of the film, we don't know what happened.

DeLillo: We're still in the dark. What we finally have are patches and shadows. It's still a mystery. There's still an element of dream-terror. And one of the terrible dreams is that our most photogenic president is murdered on film. But there's something inevitable about the Zapruder film. It had to happen this way. The moment belongs to the twentieth century, which means it had to be captured on film.

Interviewer: Can we even go further and say that part of the confusion is created by the film? After all, if the film didn't exist it would be much harder to posit a conspiracy theory.

DeLillo: I think every emotion we felt is part of that film, and certainly confusion is one of the larger ones, yes. Confusion and horror. The head shot is like some awful, pornographic moment that happens without warning in our living rooms—some truth about the world, some unspeakable activity people engage in that we don't want to know about. And after the confusion about when Kennedy is first hit, and when Connally is hit, and why the president's wife is scrambling over the seat, and simultaneous with the horror of the head shot, part of the horror, perhaps—there's a bolt of revelation. Because the head shot is the most direct kind of statement that the lethal bullet was fired from the front. Whatever the physical possibilities concerning impact and reflex, you look at this thing and wonder what's going on. Are you seeing some distortion inherent in the film medium or in your own perception of things? Are you the willing victim of some enormous lie of the state—a lie, a wish, a dream? Or, did the shot simply come from the front, as every cell in your body tells you it did?

Interviewer: From David Bell making a film about himself in *Americana* to the Führer-bunker porno film in *Running Dog*, to the filmmaker Volterra's mini-lecture in *The Names*, you return incessantly to the subject of movies. "The twentieth century is on film," you wrote in *The Names*, it's "the filmed century."

DeLillo: Film allows us to examine ourselves in ways earlier societies could not—examine ourselves, imitate ourselves, extend ourselves, reshape our reality. It permeates our lives, this double vision, and also detaches us, turns some of us into actors doing walk-throughs. In my work, film and television are often linked with disaster. Because this is one of the energies that charges the culture. TV has a sort of panting lust for bad news and calamity as long as it is visual. We've reached the point where things exist so they can be filmed and played and replayed. Some people may have had the impression that the Gulf War was made for television. And when the Pentagon censored close coverage, people became depressed. All that euphoria drifting through the country suddenly collapsed—not because we weren't winning but because they'd taken away our combat footage. Think about the images most often repeated. The Rodney King videotape or the Challenger disaster or Ruby shooting Oswald. These are the images that connect us the way Betty Grable used to connect us in her white swimsuit, looking back at us over her shoulder in the famous pinup. And they play the tape again and again and again and again. This is the world narrative, so they play it until everyone in the world has seen it.

Interviewer: Frank Lentricchia refers to you as the type of writer who believes that the shape and fate of the culture dictates the shape and fate of the self.

DeLillo: Yes, and maybe we can think about *Running Dog* in this respect. This book is not exactly about obsession—it's about the marketing of obsession. Obsession as a product that you offer to the highest bidder or the most enterprising and reckless fool, which is sort of the same thing in this particular book. Maybe this novel is a response to the war in Vietnam—this is what I'm getting at—and how the war affected the way people worked out their own strategies, how individuals conducted their own lives. There's a rampant need among the characters, a driving urge that certain characters feel to acquire the book's sacred object, a home movie made in Hitler's bunker. All the paranoia, manipulation, violence, all the sleazy desires are a form of fallout from the Vietnam experience. And in *Libra*, of course—here we have Oswald watching TV, Oswald working the bolt of his rifle, Oswald imagining that he and the president are quite similar in many ways. I see Oswald, back from Russia, as a man surrounded by promises of fulfillment—consumer fulfillment, personal fulfillment. But he's poor, unstable, cruel to his wife, barely employable—a man who has to enter his own Hollywood movie to see who he is and how he must direct his fate. This is the force of the culture and the power of the image. And this is also a story we've seen updated through the years. It's the story of the disaffected young man who suspects there are sacred emanations flowing from the media heavens and who feels the only way to enter this holy vortex is through some act of violent theater. I think Oswald was a person who lost his faith—his faith in politics and in the possibility of change—and who entered the last months of his life not very different from the media-poisoned boys who would follow.

Interviewer: In *The New York Review of Books* you were dubbed "the chief shaman of the paranoid school of American fiction." What does this title mean to you, if anything?

DeLillo: I realize this is a title one might wear honorably. But I'm not sure I've earned it. Certainly there's an element of paranoia in my work—*Libra*, yes, although not nearly so much as some people think. In this book the element of chance and coincidence may be as strong as the sense of an engineered history. History is engineered after the assassination, not before. *Running Dog* and *Great Jones Street* may also have a paranoid sheen. But I'm not particularly paranoid myself. I've drawn this element out of the air around me, and it was a stronger force in the sixties and seventies than it is now. The important thing about the paranoia in my characters is that it operates as a form of religious awe. It's something old, a leftover from some forgotten part of the soul. And the intelligence agencies that create and service this paranoia are not interesting to me as spy handlers or masters of espionage. They represent old mysteries and fascinations, ineffable things. Central intelligence. They're like churches that hold the final secrets.

Interviewer: It's been said that you have an "ostentatiously gloomy view of American society."

DeLillo: I don't agree, but I can understand how a certain kind of reader would see the gloomy side of things. My work doesn't offer the comforts of other kinds of fiction, work that suggests that our lives and our problems and our perceptions are no different today than they were fifty or sixty years ago. I don't offer comforts except those that lurk in comedy and in structure and in language, and the comedy is probably not all that soothing. But before everything, there's language. Before history and politics, there's language. And it's language, the sheer pleasure of making it and bending it and seeing it form on the page and hearing it whistle in my head—this is the thing that makes my work go. And art can be exhilarating despite the darkness—and there's certainly much darker material than mine—if the reader is sensitive to the music. What I try to do is create complex human beings, ordinary-extraordinary men and women who live in the particular skin of the late twentieth century. I try to record what I see and hear and sense around me—what I feel in the currents, the electric stuff of the culture. I think these are American forces and energies. And they belong to our time.

Interviewer: What have you been working on recently?

DeLillo: Sometime in late 1991 I started writing something new and didn't know what it would be—a novel, a short story, a long story. It was simply a piece of writing, and it gave me more pleasure than any other writing I've done. It turned into a novella, "Pafko at the Wall," and it appeared in *Harper's* about a year after I started it. At some point I decided I wasn't finished with the piece. I was sending signals into space and getting echoes back, like a dolphin or a bat. So the piece, slightly altered, is now the prologue, to a novel-in-progress, which will have a different title. And the pleasure has long since faded into the slogging reality of the no-man's-land of the long novel. But I'm still hearing the echoes.

Interviewer: Do you have any plans for after the novel-in-progress?

DeLillo: Not any specific plans. But I'm aware of the fact that time is limited. Every new novel stretches the term of the contract—let me live long enough to do one more book. How many books do we get? How much good work? The actuaries of the novel say twenty years of our best work, and after that we're beachcombing for shiny stones. I don't necessarily agree, but I'm aware of fleeting time.

Interviewer: Does that make you nervous?
DeLillo: No, it doesn't make me nervous, it just makes me want to write a little faster.

Interviewer: But you'll keep on writing?
DeLillo: I'll keep writing something, certainly.

Interviewer: I mean, you couldn't take up gardening?
DeLillo: No, no, no, no, no.

Interviewer: Handball?
DeLillo: Do you know what a Chinese killer is? It's a handball term—when you hit the ball right at the seam of the wall and the ground, and the shot is unreturnable. This used to be called a Chinese killer.

An Interview with Don DeLillo

Maria Nadotti / 1993

From *Salmagundi* 100, Fall, 1993, pp. 86–97. Translated by Peggy Boyers. Reprinted by permission.

Don DeLillo in person seems utterly different from the image of himself he has allowed to circulate in photographs. Though he is slim, modest, and mild, the photograph on the back cover of his novel Mao II, *makes him appear large, hard, imperious and slightly menacing. "Neutral" or "anonymous" are probably the correct adjectives to describe him: he has the neutrality of the person who prefers the position of observer to that of protagonist and as a consequence equips himself by choosing the only suitable means for the task, the ability to disappear, to camouflage himself, to become one among many. Therefore, he is always different, depending on what is required. His body—and even his voice—seem not to leave a trace; they tend to be forgettable, to give themselves over to being reabsorbed into the fullness from whence they came. As I will come to understand in the course of the interview, that which seems to resemble a handicap is rather a game of transformation. We can practice the game, if we apply ourselves, by projecting from ourselves a desired image, according to our pleasure: An exercise we can define as one of power relations in which the object seems to be that of distancing the possible interlocutors from oneself and of conducting the game of relations from that point. Appearing, disappearing, reappearing with another face, another 'look', he seems to be saying: "The next time we meet I'm sure you won't recognize me." And to think that all this started with my expression of surprise when we were introduced—"impossible to recognize you, I made you out to be taller"—the fault of these impossible fantasies one entertains about authors as one reads them and holds up some scrap of a photograph which is probably years old. "No, no," he says, "it's true that I've shrunk. With every book I get a little smaller. In the end there'll be nothing left."*

Q: Let's begin with one of your fundamental concerns, one which is central to a novel like *Mao II*, namely, the relationship between the individual and the crowd, the mass, especially with regard to the North American situation today.

A: Well, I think that crowds have entered our consciousness in a big way. I don't know exactly how it happens, but it's like some sort of wave of desire which crosses the oceans and continents and sends the people into the streets. In *Mao II* there are people everywhere: in the streets, on television, in stadiums, crowds of revolutionaries, crowds of mourners, different sorts of crowds. My book, in a way, is asking who is speaking to these people. Is it the writer who traditionally thought he could influence the imagination of his contemporaries or is it rather the totalitarian leader, the military man, the terrorist, those who are twisted by power and who seem capable of imposing their vision on the world, reducing the earth to a place of danger and anger. Things have changed a lot in recent years. One doesn't step onto an airplane in the same spirit as one did ten years ago: it's all different and this change has insinuated itself into our consciousness with the same force with which it insinuated itself into the visions of Beckett or Kafka.

There's something about a crowd which suggests a sort of implicit panic, even when it's a friendly crowd. There's something menacing and violent about a mass of people which makes us think of the end of individuality, whether they are gathered around a military leader or around a holy man.

The photographic image is a kind of crowd in itself, a jumble of impressions very different in kind from a book in which the printed lines follow one another in a linear order. There's something in the image that seems to collide with the very idea of individual identity. Here I'm getting into very subjective territory. But let's return to the writer. I don't think that a writer can allow himself the luxury of separating himself from the crowd, even if he is by definition a person who spends much of his life alone in a room in the company of a typewriter, paper and pen. It is indispensable to be fully involved in contemporary life, to be part of the crowd, of the clash of voices. Just as I was finishing *Mao II* I was immersed in reading the John Cheever diaries. On one page, Cheever tells what he saw happen one evening in New York during a baseball game. A player hits the ball into the stands. Forty people go after the ball, all trying to grab it. Cheever says that the job of the writer is not to describe the thoughts of an adulterous woman standing at the window watching the rain streak the glass. The writer, he says, should understand those forty people trying to get the baseball, understand the other ten or twenty thousand people who leave the stadium when the game is over. "Moral judgments embodied in a migratory vastness." For me it was strange. I mean, perhaps it was because I was finishing *Mao II* just then that the words struck me so forcefully, above all perhaps because they came from a writer like Cheever who had spent his entire professional life trying to understand the adulterous woman. I suppose that somehow he gave voice to an intuition which I had simply followed, that is, an attempt to place myself in the midst of a crowd.

Q: At what point would you place this intuition? When did it become necessary to forget about the woman and her ruminations on adultery in order to occupy yourself with the masses?
A: It all began with a photograph. I happened to come across a picture of a mass wedding, a ceremony which took place in an industrial warehouse in South Korea. Sixteen thousand people were involved. It was one of those mass weddings of the Unification Church, an organized, orderly crowd. From that point I began thinking about the psychology of the crowd, of the obliteration of distinctions, of how people lose themselves in the multitude, of the need to belong to the multitude. This made me reflect immediately on the juxtaposition between the regimented crowd and the writer who is trying to understand this phenomenon, who lives alone, who could be a recluse like Bill Gray (the main protagonist of *Mao II*), and who keeps himself secluded, away from the roar of our culture, away from the world of images. So that's how I thought of my character, a very solitary writer who agrees to have his picture taken. This is how he gives away what little power he has over his own life. That's where I began: why does he accept the role of photographic subject? What relation does he have to those who photograph him, etc.? Well, I don't know if I've succeeded in answering all these questions.

Q: How much self-reference is there in your novel? Is Bill Gray a stand-in for Don DeLillo, or have I allowed myself to be influenced by your reputation as a person who doesn't appear very often in public?
A: No, Bill Gray is not modeled on my life or work. I'm not a solitary person. Gray does not resemble me, is not my age and doesn't write like me—well, maybe a little. He doesn't lead my sort of life, nor does he share my personal history. Perhaps we have a few thoughts in common; perhaps as writers we have the same doubts about ourselves. But if I'd wanted to I could have created a much more autobiographical figure. Instead, I wanted to make him a character like any other, no different from Karen or from Scott (two other characters of *Mao II*). I felt much more comfortable writing from

Karen's point of view than from Bill's. Bill gave me a ton of trouble. It took me an eternity to enter his consciousness; while with Karen I was at home from the start.

Q: Do you mind if we talk a bit about women and their relationship to men? In *Mao II* there are three relevant passages which interest me. Let me read them to you: "Middle aged women go generally unnoticed." "When is it that women began to photograph men?" "Men have a certain tendency to disappear." All three passages revolve around the theme of seeing and being seen and the dynamic which fits the masculine to the feminine. Do they have to do with some of the transformations which have taken place and which are still taking place in American society?
A: I believe that some classes of people are invisible. Middle-aged women belong to this group more than older women do and certainly more than younger women do. Therefore it's an age in which women begin to feel themselves invisible in a way. I don't think this happens to men.

Q: Why does it happen to women?
A: Because women are so often the objects of attention, at so many levels. Whether they're in a street car, walking down a street or sitting in a restaurant, men look at them constantly and force them at some level to become self-conscious objects of scrutiny. What I mean is that we are all of us made up not only of muscle, brains and blood, but also of the things which others tell us and of the things others see in us. This is why I believe that it must be very disturbing to become suddenly invisible.

Q: Has Brita, who is hired to photograph Bill Gray in *Mao II*, perhaps found a way to escape invisibility by reversing the terms and becoming herself a perceiving subject rather than a perceived object?
A: Reversing the terms? In a sense yes, I think so. She is in this way exercising a certain control over people. In the case of the book, moreover, she is photographing a man. When is it that women began to photograph men? I don't know. I don't even know why Gray asks himself this question. Maybe he just wants to have fun; maybe it's just a line used to create a relaxed jokey atmosphere. But when *did* it occur, anyway? And was it important? In short, did the world change when women began watching men, becoming spectators rather than objects?

Q: But is it the case at this point that women, in the US at least, have begun to look?

A: Yes, but should we say that women have begun to look at men or that they have begun to LOOK? This is the real question.

Q: And your answer would be—?

A: To tell you the truth I am more persuaded by the second hypothesis. I think that the basic thing is that women have begun to put their eyes behind cameras. Whatever is on the other side that becomes the object will now be seen in a different way from the way it would be seen otherwise, especially if the object on the other side of the view finder is a man.

Q: Let's get back to the relationship between individuals and the masses. What need is it that propels the single person to lose himself in the multitude? Is it his need for that someone else to take care of him? Is it the need to free himself of responsibility?

A: I think that it has to do with something deeper. What you're saying addresses only part of the problem. The need is not only to abandon responsibility, but to abandon one's self, to escape the weight of being and to exist within a collective chorus—to lose not only one's own identity but one's own language, to be in the midst of a million people who are screaming the same word, always the same word forever. For some it amounts to a sort of ecstasy. What is it? A path of escape from pain, from regret, from sadness and from other things.

Q: Does it scare you?

A: Yes, it's frightening, but it is also interesting and can be beautiful to behold. Think of Mecca. I've never been there, of course, but I've seen photographs of the place and of those who make pilgrimages there: they've struck me in their extreme beauty. There is an enormous structure, the Kaaba, a great black cube. The pilgrims run around it, thousands of people running in a circle around a gigantic black cube. It's fantastic.

Q: Apparently.

A: Yes, apparently, and I might even like to run with them.

Q: In *Mao II* there is a sentence which goes something like this: the writer is half terrorist. Ideally, he would like to influence people's conscience, but he fails to do so. Today only an act of terrorism succeeds in changing people's lives. Do you miss the power which the act of writing seems to have lost? Do you envy those who find power in violence? Or am I pushing your words too far?

A: No, I don't think that it has to do with envy or terror. I want to answer you honestly because your question is complicated. There would be a latent anger—and I don't mean violence—in what a lot of writers do and—you know—it's an anger which is often neither recognized nor understood. It's like investigating a type of imagination which is the opposite yet in some ways the same as one's own. I can't and shouldn't mention the names of other writers. This is my way of seeing and it is dictated principally by the way I am made, but when I wrote *Mao II* I had the sensation of having arrived at a point where the gains that terrorists were realizing through violence had a way of reducing the ground traditionally possible for writers. It doesn't only have to do with terror, but with another vast arena: the news. The news is fiction, the news is the new narrative—particularly, the dark news, the tragic news. I think that from this kind of news people find a kind of narrative with a tragic stamp which in another time they found in fiction. I don't know exactly why this is. Maybe it depends on the fact that television, and its way of delivering the news, is so powerful. Or maybe it has to do simply with the spirit which has entered our consciousness, a sort of apocalyptic sense of things. I imagine people, individuals, watching their t.v. screens and having their own private apocalypses because right in front of them they have vivid images of real earthquakes and the like. Something is happening which has to do with the displacement of desire. You know in the past the great leaders had the imagination to create an empire of enormous spatial dimensions. Now they dream in terms of computer chips. Look, everything has become miniaturized, including desire. People—at least in the U.S.— have located or rather identified their requirements by narrowing their lives, their identities, their personal needs and specific desires. One speaks of groups, of ever more discrete and separate entities: the elderly, the teachers, the lesbians, and so on. But I imagine that the moment is about to arrive in which there will be so many cable t.v. channels, hundreds perhaps, from which each one of us will be able to select the program that responds to our own particular interests by pressing a button. If you're an insurance agent you'll find the half hour of news relative to your specific field, and probably you'll be in the news yourself. This is the direction in which we're headed.

Q: Let's move to what seems to be at the base of the whole matter. What relationship do you see between consumerism, the indifference of the masses and the loss of personal identity?

A: Well, I see a relationship between consumerism and the homeless people I describe in *Mao II* who live in Tompkins Square, New York City, who live in refrigerator boxes and television boxes. If you could write slogans for nations similar to those invented by advertisers for their products the slogan for the US would be "Consume or die." The consequence of not having the power to consume is that you end up living in the streets. Through products and advertising people attain impersonal identity. I've written about the power of the image in earlier books. It's as if fantasies and dreams could become realized with the help of the entire consumer imagination that surrounds us, a form of self-realization through products.

Q: How would you define your books from a literary point of view?
A: They're novels, just novels.

Q: Do you approve of their being described as post-modern novels? How do you react to such a formulation?
A: I don't react. But I'd prefer not to be labeled. I'm a novelist, period. An American novelist. When *Libra* came out some people started to talk about facts, fiction and writing, about documentary writing and so on. But *Libra* is just a novel. Look, Homer wrote about real people around 4,000 years ago and we continue to do the same things except we call it a novel. Right?

Q: And what do you think of that strange neologism, "faction"?
A: It's terrible; it's outdated. It was new a few years ago and then it disappeared. The term isn't worth anything. It's stupid.

Q: Are there American writers whose work seems close to yours?
A: Robert Stone, Thomas Pynchon, Paul Auster, Cormac McCarthy, William Gaddis and others. And there are some younger writers who are taking fiction out of the realm of the domestic and into that of history: Richard Powers, Joanna Scott, David Foster Wallace, Jonathan Franzen, to name just a few.

Q: Tell me about Oliver Stone's *JFK*. What do you think of it? Were you at all involved in the film?

A: No, I had nothing to do with it. Another company had bought the option on *Libra*, but then they never gathered the necessary money to make a film. Oliver Stone simply found another book and made *JFK*.

Q: Did you like it?
A: Regardless of his vigorous imagination I don't think it was anything but an example of a particular type of nostalgia: the nostalgia for a master plan, the conspiracy which explains absolutely everything.

Q: But the film has at least reopened the case.
A: Some people think the movie raised the level of political discourse and others think it prompted the government to open secret files. This is good. But what we perceive from this experience, more than anything else, is the enormous power of commercial movie making. Many excellent nonfiction books about the assassination came and went without a murmur. It reminds us that in America today you have to spend forty million dollars to make a point.

Q: Could we talk about something you've discussed more than once in your work, namely, the writer's special experience of time?
A: Whoever is writing a novel has a very acute sense of time. Why? Because when you begin to write a novel you know it may take years to finish. It's not like writing a short story, a dramatic work or an article. We're talking about three or four years in the case of *Libra*, for example. So there's one dominant preoccupation. It's not only that you want to write a marvelous book, but you want to finish it before you die. This is something I felt even when I wrote my first novel, and I was only 29 years old when I started. It happens with every book. It becomes a race.

Q: Is there a sense in which a book can become the enemy of its author?
A: It's a struggle, a struggle against the book which won't reveal itself, which refuses to reveal its mysteries on schedule. Books reveal their mysteries in their own good time. You just have to wait.

Q: And what about the physical circumstances in which you write?
A: I use a manual typewriter, an old typewriter on a table, a dictionary, a few notes. Everything right there. I work every morning until around one, then I try to work at least another hour or two in the afternoon and after a while I

begin to get the rhythm and the days start to become satisfying. You begin to realize that you're into another book, another world.

There's a physical element in the act of writing. While I'm writing I walk a lot. I get up, I go to the end of the hall, I look out the window. Finally, I go back to my room and sit down again. I don't use a word processor because I like the feeling of touching the paper, of making changes with a pencil or a pen, of saving old pages that one can return to in a year or so.

I save every note and this, too, is part of the tactile dimension of writing. It's very important for me to keep discarded pages because they form a kind of history of my efforts. And they're connected with the sense of a familiar physical surrounding. When I go away somewhere and try to write it takes me days to become accustomed to the new environment. It's a shock not to have my own table, my own walls, certain pictures, photographs, objects, books. It's like being lost in space and I need a long time to settle in. There is about writing a deep, very radical sense of habit, of one's own miniscule idiosyncrasies, that transports us to the realm of imagination.

Q: Do you think you could get used to a computer?
A: No, I need the sound of the keys, the keys of a manual typewriter. The hammers striking the page. I like to see the words, the sentences, as they take shape. It's an aesthetic issue: when I work I have a sculptor's sense of the shape of the words I'm making. I use a machine with larger than average letters: the bigger the better.

Q: Does your reluctance to appear in public have something to do with an uneasiness about being reduced to some sort of commodity?
A: Undoubtedly this is one of the reasons. I don't want to become familiar.

Q: Would you say you have an inclination towards invisibility?
A: I guess you could put it that way. There's an idea in *Mao II*: When you look at your own photograph you can react in two ways: you can either decide that your life should follow the direction of that image or you can alienate yourself from it. Do you want to look like your photograph or do you want to escape it? It's an existential question.

Q: And usually you distance yourself. Let's talk about the title of *Mao II* and the illustration you chose for the cover, "New Series 1972–74," by Andy Warhol. In the novel, history and politics join with art, but above all with the principle of repetition, of artificiality, of fiction and with a taste for necrophilia—all dear to Warhol.

A: What Warhol succeeded in achieving was to take an image and make it fluctuate freely, liberating it from history: a man who is immersed in wars and revolutions becomes a sort of icon painted on a flat surface. In the same way that soup is packaged, Warhol packages his Mao's, his Marilyn Monroe's and his Elvis Presley's. He simply repeats the images. Interesting work, and judging from its extraordinary reception, perhaps a little frightening as well.

By that I mean that through repetition the artist obliterates distinctions: when the images are identical to each other consumerism and the mass production of art in their most explicit form take over.

Q: Have you ever written for the newspapers or magazines?
A: Only rarely.

Q: The line between literature and information, as you've said yourself, is becoming finer and finer. Many of the most beautiful "novels" of recent years have been written by journalists describing reality: Ryszard Kapuscinski, Amitav Ghosh, Bill Buford.
A: The fact is that I don't want to be a part of the story I'm telling. I need fictional characters as a mediating truth. Maybe if I were 20 years old, I'd want to be a journalist and, even if I were later to become a novelist, I'd want to start out as a journalist.

Q: Why?
A: Because it gives you a reliable sense of reality and of the world. A reliable illusion.

Q: And what would you want to write about?
A: About war.

Q: Real wars or the kinds of wars that are battled out in the home?
A: If you had asked me this question a few years ago I would have answered, "in the Middle East," because I was very interested in the events occurring in that area, and would have liked to go to Beirut or Iran. Instead I wrote *Libra*.

The American Strangeness: An Interview with Don DeLillo

Gerald Howard / 1997

From *The Hungry Mind Review*, #47, 1997, pp. 13–16. Reprinted by permission.

In 1983 Don DeLillo published in *Rolling Stone* a powerful meditation on the meaning(s) of the assassination of John Kennedy twenty years after the event. In it he describes a poker game that took place in a Manhattan high-rise on April 4, 1968, the evening of yet another shattering assassination, the shooting of Martin Luther King, Jr., in Memphis. As sirens began to echo around the city, one of the card players, white, began speaking as if possessed in a deeply resonant Negro voice and would or could not stop, disconcerting all the players. It's a perfect found DeLillo moment, and his comment on it is equally perfect: "How strange it was to be an American."

Indeed. We are only beginning to grasp how strange. In his ten previous novels Don DeLillo has been constructing ever more haunting geographies of American strangeness, capturing with his restless, acute, and unflagging intelligence the floating moods of a country unsure, it seems, of almost everything besides its own dread and uncertainty. In the process he has created a body of work extravagantly and rightly admired by critics and his fellow novelists—and by an increasingly wide readership eager to rise to the challenge of his fiction.

On October 3, 1997, Scribners will publish DeLillo's new novel, *Underworld*, a massive, 833-page—let's get the word out of the way, there's no avoiding it and no reason to try—masterpiece. Like some fantastically all-seeing, all-knowing literary search engine, he probes the postwar American psyche for the source of our dis-ease, and locates it in the nuclear threat that has shadowed our every mood and action since Hiroshima. *Underworld* is a Book of Days for America's nuclear age, for our very, very Strange Days, and it comes at the perfect post–Cold War moment. As Klara Sax, a visionary artist and one of the book's two central characters, muses, "Now that power is in shatters and tatters and now that those Soviet borders don't even exist in the same way, I think we understand, we look back, we see ourselves more clearly and them as well."

Although *Underworld* can fairly be called epic in scope and while it might well serve as a textbook for the study of postmodern literary techniques, it feels intimate throughout. It is certainly DeLillo's most personal book in its use of and allegiance to the Bronx of his boyhood, the borough from which the book's four main characters emerge into history: Klara Sax; Nick Shay, an executive in the richly metaphorical business of waste management; his brother Matt Shay, an atomic intellectual; and the teacher Albert Bronzini, Klara's former husband and Matt's former chess coach. Around them orbit a cast of characters partly real—J. Edgar Hoover, Sergei Eisenstein, Lenny Bruce—and partly invented—Sister Edgar, the Texas Highway Killer. Threaded throughout the proceedings, in a manner not dissimilar to the search for V. in Thomas Pynchon's novel, is the quest for the most significant home run ball in baseball history. It ends in a brutal death and a moving transfiguration in the South Bronx— one of the few convincing manifestations of grace, in the precise Catholic sense, in American fiction since Flannery O'Connor.

Don DeLillo is the pure product of New York City. Raised in the Arthur Avenue section of the Bronx, he was educated in Catholic schools—Cardinal Hayes High School and Fordham University—and for a time worked, like Salman Rushdie, for Ogilvy and Mather as an advertising copywriter. But since the late sixties he has done nothing professionally but write novels, essays, short stories, and plays. Literally nothing: like his peers William Gaddis and Thomas Pynchon he has never taught creative writing, given lectures, attended writers conferences, sat on discussion panels, reviewed books, or participated in the other extraneous activities of a contemporary literary career. His purity is exemplary, and, in the way it forces readers to apprehend his work, aesthetically shrewd.

He does, however, sit for the occasional interview. When this publication asked me to do this piece, I realized that in a way I had been talking in my head to Don DeLillo since 1973, when I was captured by the very first sentence of his first novel, *Americana* ("Then we came to the end of another dull and lurid year"). I felt then, and I still feel now, that whatever he writes is speaking to me and for me. Through the seventies and early eighties I immediately bought his novels in hardcover first editions when this constituted, for me, a major outlay of discretionary income. In 1988 a delightful series of circumstances allowed me to be the editor at Viking for

Libra, his most commercially successful book to date; it doesn't get any better than this. We share Catholic, outer-borough backgrounds and a love for and fascination with New York City, movies, and jazz. This interview took place on a late spring day in Don DeLillo's home just north of New York City—not terribly far from the Bronx neighborhood and the now-vanished Manhattan stadium where key sections of *Underworld* take place.

Howard: The last time you sat for an interview, in 1993 for the *Paris Review* Writers at Work series, you had just published a novella, *Pafko at the Wall*, which then turned into the long prologue to the book we have now. When and how did you first become aware of the extraordinary coincidence of the two "Shots Heard Round the World," Bobby Thomson's epochal 1951 home run, and the explosion of a Soviet nuclear device?

DeLillo: I was reading the newspaper one morning in October 1991, and there was a story about the fortieth anniversary of a legendary ball game between the Giants and Dodgers, the third game of the play-offs, which the Giants won dramatically on a ninth inning home run by Bobby Thomson. I read it and forgot all about it, but several weeks later began to think about it again in a different context—historical. It seemed to be a kind of unrepeatable event, the kind of thing that binds people in a certain way. Not only people who were at the ballpark, but fans in general and even nonfans who were not necessarily interested in the baseball implications. There was a sense, at least for me, that this was the last such binding event that mainly involved jubilation rather than disaster of some sort. Anyway, I went to the library and found a reel of microfilm for the *New York Times* of the following day, October 4, 1951. I didn't know what I was looking for, but what I found was two headlines, symmetrically matched. It was like fitting together two pieces of ancient pottery. One headline concerned the ball game, "Giants Capture Pennant" and so on. The other headline concerned an atomic test that the Soviet Union had set off in Kazhakstan. Very few details were given, but the two bold matching headlines caused a sort of pause in me. There was a strong sense of the power of history, and this is what got me started thinking about the Cold War.

Howard: Well, my only caveat to that is that there wasn't much jubilation in Brooklyn that day. My father, a regular attendee at Ebbets Field, wore the scars from that game like a stigmata.

DeLillo: That's right, of course. But I think that what flowed from the event was the picture of Thomson circling the bases and the celebrations that arose spontaneously throughout the city, excluding Brooklyn. Very soon, perhaps the next day in the *Daily News*, this home run became known as the "Shot Heard Round the World," which connected it again, eerily and coincidentally, with the Soviet nuclear test.

Howard: *Underworld* provokes a number of simpleminded factual questions that I know are completely unworthy of me, and I am going to confine myself to one. Is it true that J. Edgar Hoover, Frank Sinatra, and Jackie Gleason were in a box together at that game?

DeLillo: Yes, it is true, they were at the game, and Toots Shor as well. They were cronies and they met that morning at Toots Shor's restaurant, more or less accidentally, and Sinatra had four tickets which had been given to him by Leo Durocher, the Giants manager. They got into a limousine and went up to the Polo Grounds. Hoover is, of course, the odd man out in this little congregation—seemingly. But in fact he was an avid sportsman, at least at some level, and went often to the race track. He did frequent the Stork Club and Toots Shor's restaurant, and liked being around celebrities. So once I found out that Hoover had been at the game, it struck me with the force of revelation, because it meant that I had someone in the Polo Grounds who was intimately connected to what had happened in Kazhakstan. And I was able to blend these two events naturally and seamlessly.

Howard: The structure and the overall conception of *Underworld* is exceptionally inventive and unconventional. The general drift of the book moves backward in time, from our ambiguous post–Cold War present to the intimate clarity of life in a Bronx neighborhood in the fifties. This reverse trajectory is traced by all of the book's major characters. The unity of the book, its vast tapestry of characters, settings, and episodes, is created not so much by plot as by a weave of thematic connections. I'd like to ask you how this conception of the book evolved.

DeLillo: Once I set the structure and once I figured it out, I took it for granted and haven't really thought much about it. But it occurred to me recently that in a curious way it duplicates the countdown voice we associate with a nuclear test—ten, nine, eight, seven . . .

When I finished the prologue and started Part One, I began the narrative on the day following the game. See, I had no sense at this point that I wanted to create an enormous separation in time between the Prologue and the beginning of the book proper. So what is now Part Six was originally Part One, and I wrote twenty pages, was having a wonderful time describing street games in the Bronx—and realized, finally, that this was all wrong. And it wasn't until I finished twenty or twenty-five pages that I decided I had to do something drastic. And then the idea of a Part One that begins roughly forty years after the Prologue occurred to me. Then I realized that I would have to work backwards, toward the day of the ball game. What may seem obvious to most people looking at the book struck me with the force of enormous revelation, as obvious things often do when you are working on a piece of fiction, particularly something of this length.

Howard: This is entirely parenthetical, but another thing I thought of when I was coming over here was *Magic Mountain*. I remember finishing that book, and at the end Thomas Mann basically says in an afterword, "Thanks for finishing it. Now go back and read it again, because now you can appreciate what I have been doing, since I work with this leitmotif method." And that is precisely the feeling that I had about *Underworld* as I went back through it the second time to prepare for this interview. This time around I was clued to the idea that this wasn't a book that was structured in conventional narrative terms—although it does have plenty of narrative elements.
DeLillo: Someone finishing *Underworld* said, "This is not a book you can read, this is a book you have to re-read." I haven't read *Magic Mountain*, but that is an interesting statement Mann made, which I came across, coincidentally, just recently—that you can't read my work, you have to reread it.

Howard: Well, the first thing that people are going to notice about *Underworld* is its length. The second is its ambition—it aspires to nothing less than a re-imagining of the American experience in the nuclear age. The short list of books that similarly attempt to grapple with the subterranean history of postwar American life, notably *Gravity's Rainbow* (Pynchon), *The Recognitions* (Gaddis), and perhaps *Infinite Jest* (David Foster Wallace), is stacked with behemoths. What is it about that task that demands such length and complexity?

DeLillo: Maybe the answer is contained in the question. The last half century has been an enormously complex period—a strange spin-out experience, filled with danger and change. The novel is a very open form. It will accommodate large themes and whole landscapes of experience. The novel is here, the novel exists to give us a form that is fully equal to the sweeping realties of a given period. The novel expands, contracts, becomes essaylike, floats in pure consciousness—it gives the writer what he needs to produce a book that duplicates, a book that models the rich, dense, and complex weave of actual experience. The novel goads the writer into surpassing himself.

Howard: It seems to me that *Underworld* proposes almost a new understanding of history—what history is, how people experience it. It is different from your earlier work. One of the most quoted lines from your novels is the line from *Libra*: "History is the sum total of the things they're not telling us." *Libra* dealt with aspects of conspiracy and paranoia. This book, in contrast, is pretty free of conspiracy. There is no sense of some vast agency or Other pulling the strings. There is a sense of togetherness under a nuclear shadow, and that to understand the history of the post-Bomb years we have to understand how that shadow manifested itself in every nook and cranny of our lives.

DeLillo: That's right. What is the role of high technology in creating the way we think and feel? The paranoia in *Libra* flows from unknowable plots being worked out in hidden corners. In *Underworld* it comes from the huge overarching presence of highly complex and interconnected technological systems. There's a feeling I have that people become more pliable, that people lose a measure of conviction as technology becomes more powerful and more sophisticated. I think it's interesting and curious that the Heaven's Gate group was computer-proficient. Against this technical skill we pose their childlike innocence and superstition. Maybe it's not coincidental. I think there is something in *Underworld* that moves in this direction. Of course, the novel ends in cyberspace. This is a realization of a sense in the book that all technology refers to the Bomb. Because what we see in those final scenes is a series of hydrogen bomb explosions on a special Web site. There's a religious aspect to this and again I think of the Heaven's Gate group and their mass suicide. There's a false faith. Maybe they thought they were going into cyberspace. The worship of technology ends in the paranoid spaces of the computer net.

Howard: *Underworld* draws its title from the brilliantly imagined rediscovered film of Eisenstein, *Unterwelt*. It joins other visual documents, actual and fabricated, of the twentieth century in your work, the autobiographical road movie by David Bell in *Americana*, the allegedly pornographic film made in Hitler's bunker from *Running Dog*, the Zapruder film whose footage haunts *Libra* and also *Underworld*. Why does film stand so conspicuously at the center of your work rather than books?
DeLillo: Because this is the age of images, I suppose, and much that is different about our time can be traced to the fact that we are on film, a reality that did not shape, instruct, and haunt previous cultures. I suppose film gives us a deeply self-conscious sense, but beyond that it's simply such a prevalent fact of contemporary life that I don't think any attempt to understand the way we live and the way we think and the way we feel about ourselves can proceed without a deep consideration of the power of the image.

Howard: I really admire the way the Eisenstein film unites so many strands of meaning and imagery in *Underworld*. To take just two: A viewer of the film remarks that "the theme deals on some level with people living in the shadows," which I think is a clear statement of your novel's anatomy of the nuclear shadows characters live under. And its parade of haunting grotesques anticipates the horrible fate of the downwinders from America's nuclear test sites and the inhabitants of the Museum of the Misshapen in Kazhakstan. I think it's in this film that the method of the book is fully realized.
DeLillo: The film supplies a Russian presence right in the middle of the book, the almost literal middle of the book, and it also explores a kind of gradation from the political repression of the Stalin era to something that in a way is deeper and more personal, a kind of sexual self-repression. Eisenstein figures into this and so does J. Edgar Hoover. And so does the mention of the old radio program "The F.B.I. in Peace and War," and the theme music of that program from Prokofiev, "The Love of Three Oranges," which is played at the Radio City Music Hall during the showing of *Unterwelt*. And these things curiously invent themselves. One doesn't have to work very hard to establish this sort of thematic consistency. A theme will insist on its own development.

Howard: It seems inevitable that the nuclear threat would serve as a focal point once again for a novel of yours. *End Zone* was an earlier, more manic excursion into atomic anxiety. *Underworld*, for all its moments of comic genius, is a relatively sober book with a gravitas and a scope that is absent from *End Zone*. What sort of distance do you think you and the country have traveled since 1973?

DeLillo: I think the country has entered a curious time warp. Time moves faster, memory is more or less obliterated, events seem to repeat themselves endlessly. And I guess the distance I traveled from *End Zone* is substantial but I don't think I can provide clear coordinates. You become a serious novelist by living long enough.

Howard: Let's talk about Nick Shay and your other characters for a while. Because I'm a native outer-borough New Yorker myself, perhaps, I found the material set in the Bronx of your childhood and the present day magical and moving and terrifically evocative. One of the dialectics that powers *Underworld* is that between the urban neighborhood and the larger world, the classic urban trajectory. You yourself have made that journey and so have Bronx-born literary figures like E. L. Doctorow and Richard Price. I am wondering how much of yourself you put into the rendering of Nick Shay, Matthew Shay, Klara Sax.

DeLillo: Well, certainly the background is the same. They are fictional characters. They are not drawn directly from real people, but the Bronx episodes in Part Six particularly were written out of a sense of intimate knowledge. Something I discovered after I finished writing the book, as I was reading the proofs, is that much of the book is nearly saturated with compound words, hyphenated words, many of them which I invented or grafted together. In Part Six, suddenly the language is a bit different. It's a bit simpler. It's more visceral. And it occurs to me that this is what a writer does to transcend the limitations of his background. He does it through language, obviously. He writes himself into the larger world. He opens himself to the entire culture. He becomes, in short, an American—the writer equivalent of his immigrant parents and grandparents. And so there are two sets of language in this book. The difference between them isn't very stark but in fact a sort of journey is detectable, solely in sentences and pacing and word choice, between the Bronx of Part Six and the larger environment that surrounds it.

Howard: Your ear for that street speech is absolutely perfect and it constituted for me a kind of time machine back to that time and place. I'm positive that those speech patterns could not be discovered today, except maybe in some very remote Italian-American pocket of Brooklyn or the Bronx or conceivably Staten Island.

DeLillo: Yes, it's extraordinary what memory can summon. The farther back I went, it seemed the clearer my sense of the way people spoke and dressed and the way things looked.

Howard: By a happy coincidence, I finished Philip Roth's really terrific new novel, *American Pastoral,* the other night and I'm struck by its affinities with the Bronx section of *Underworld.* Roth's memories of Newark are just as eidetic and encyclopedic as yours of Arthur Avenue. The valence is different, though. Where he is angry, you are saddened by the terrible betrayal of the American promise represented by the social disaster that has been visited on these areas. Have you read the book yet?

DeLillo: I have, yes, and it's a very strong book. Of course the Newark passages are filled with a kind of rage and I think this is the major note in the book and it's very powerful.

Howard: Just to follow that for a second, there's no sociological cause and effect proposed between the American obsession with the Cold War and the malign neglect of the cities in *Underworld,* but the parallels are unmistakable. Was the near death of the Bronx and Newark as clear a cost of the Cold War as, say, the devastating pollution of certain Soviet cities?

DeLillo: In the book there's a wasted section of the South Bronx called the Wall. It's an area outside the reach of basic services such as water and electricity. And these passages are set around the time of the fall of the Berlin Wall. There is certainly no explicit connection. There is a kind of shadow, a whisper. And there are themes of weapons and waste. The beautiful, expensive, nobly named weapons systems. And then the waste, many types of waste, and the Wall is a particular part of the waste—the part that includes human lives.

Howard: In an earlier interview, you were speaking about the urban scenes in *Great Jones Street,* and you stated, "A writer may describe the ugliness and pain in graphic terms but he can also try to find the dignity and significance in ruined parts of the city in the people he sees there." This feels to me to be a conscious anticipation of the present-day Bronx sections of *Underworld,* particularly the Puerto Rican sections. These scenes and the final one, with the death and transfiguration of Esmeralda and Sister Edgar and your very Catholic conception of cyberspace, have a remarkable effect on one's understanding of the 800 pages that precede them. It's almost as if the reader would not know what the book means without them. This is an achievement and a gamble. Were you aware of the gamble you were taking?

DeLillo: Mainly I was trying to survive, day by day. There's a strong element of faith involved when a writer works on a book of this length—his faith in what will be revealed to him as the months and years pass. A book this size does not reveal itself except in stages. I had no idea, for example, that the death of Esmeralda would end up so near the finish. It was originally part of an early chapter. You wait for things to show themselves. And when they do, it's exhilarating. Was I aware of the gamble? I wanted it. I went looking for it. That's why I wrote the book.

Howard: I think your lifelong allegiance to Father Joyce has paid off splendidly.

DeLillo: Mailer calls him Doctor Joyce. You and I know that he's a priest.

Howard: I'm struck by your generosity and your empathy in writing about artists in other mediums, especially visual artists. Warhol is a major inspiration and influence in *Mao II* and I felt that the painter Klara Sax is clearly a spiritual kin to Sullivan, the sculptress muse in *Americana*. Where does your feeling for art and artists come from? Have you associated with them much?

DeLillo: I have a few friends who are painters, but I think it's mainly one of the major effects of having grown up in New York City. It's simply the time I spent at the Museum of Modern Art and at a half dozen repertory movie theatres looking mainly at European films in the late fifties and early sixties. There's jazz in *Underworld*, too, and that would be the third element in my personal trinity—of abstract expressionism, foreign films, and jazz. These things were probably stronger influences on my sensibility than anything I read.

Howard: One of the particular excellences of *Underworld* is the way you get downtown New York in the seventies absolutely right. It was such an interesting period in American art and American sensibility. Were you, to use a shopworn phrase, a "downtown" person in those years or were you just picking up signals?

DeLillo: A little of both. Downtown is where things lay hidden, waiting for people to find them. And one of the hidden things, not only downtown, is the rooftop world—the water towers, gardens, architectural ornaments—and this is the world I tried to explore in Part Four, in the rooftop summer sequences. And of course the fact that Klara Sax is a painter and sculptor helped me see Manhattan in those terms.

Howard: I remember coming out of college in 1972 and sort of discovering Soho and areas south. There was the sense that something was going on, but it was hidden. You'd be walking along a fairly deserted street and you'd hear music from a loft, and you'd think, "I want to be up there." And eventually I did get up there. Soho was a widely shared cultural secret that had its own code.

DeLillo: And the code was largely architectural, contained in the great cast-iron buildings.

Howard: This is a complete shot in the dark, but have you ever seen any theatrical productions by Robert Wilson? Because *Underworld* is the closest thing to *Einstein on the Beach* that I can imagine in prose.

DeLillo: Well, that's one I haven't seen. I did see a production of *Alcestis* in Cambridge and it was quite interesting. I am not aware that there is any connection between his work and mine. I will say this, though: *Einstein on the Beach* is a title I wish I'd thought of first.

Howard: As you know, the part of the book that really floored me is the psychic history of the Cuban Missile Crisis in the form of a series of monologues delivered over its duration by Lenny Bruce. From my point of view you don't so much imitate or represent Bruce as channel him. It's a beautiful example of hipster hysteria, irony, scorn, and terror, mixed in precise Brucian proportions. Did you ever actually catch his act?

DeLillo: Just once. There was a place not far from where I lived. It was a club in a hotel, called the Den in the Duane, in Murray Hill of all places. I think Lenny Bruce was a very strong influence on the culture and deserves recognition at the level of Ginsberg and Burroughs and Kerouac. Although of course he was different—he was not a beatnik, he was a hipster. But the things he released into the culture were important.

Howard: You present a paradox to your admirers. In your work you describe the literary vocation with a keen sense of comic futility. I'm thinking of the obsessively unpublished writer Edward B. Fenig in *Great Jones Street*—one of my favorite characters of yours—and the pop culture theorist Murray Jay Siskind in *White Noise*. In *Libra* you suggest that our greatest experimental novelists have been trumped by the Warren Commission Report, and *Mao II* proposes that terrorists have replaced novelists as the master shapers of our common narrative. And yet in your eleven novels and especially, I believe, in *Underworld*, you offer your readers each and every one of the consolations of literature, including a moral and intellectual purchase on our inchoate and unnerving recent history. How aware are you of this contradiction? Does it energize you?

DeLillo: Well, it was a relief not to have a writer in this book, yes. The writer has lost a great deal of his influence, and he is situated now, if anywhere, on the margins of the culture. But isn't this where he belongs? How could it be any other way? And in my personal view this is a perfect place to observe what's happening at the dead center of things. I particularly have always had a kind of endgame sensibility when it comes to writing serious fiction. Before I ever published a novel, this is how I felt about it—that I was writing for a small audience that could disappear at any minute, and not only was this not a problem, it was a kind of solution. It justified what I wrote and it narrowed expectations in a healthy way. I am not particularly distressed by the state of fiction or the role of the writer. The more marginal, perhaps ultimately the more trenchant and observant and finally necessary he'll become.

Exile on Main Street: Don DeLillo's Undisclosed Underworld

David Remnick / 1997

From *The New Yorker*, September 15, 1997, pp. 42–48. Reprinted by permission; © 1997 David Remnick. All rights reserved.

In the spring of 1988, the editors of the New York *Post* sent a pair of photographers to New Hampshire with instructions to find J. D. Salinger and take his picture. If the phrase "take his picture" had any sense of violence or, at least, violation left in it at all, if it still retained the undertone of certain peoples who are convinced that a photographer threatens them with the theft of their souls, then it applied here. There is no mystery why the *Post* pursued its prey. For whatever reasons (and one presumes they are not happy reasons), Salinger stopped publishing long ago—his last story, "Hapworth 16, 1924," appeared in the *New Yorker* in 1965—and he has lived a reclusive life ever since. His withdrawal became for journalists a story demanding resolution, intervention, and exposure. Inevitably, the *Post* got its man. The journalists took Salinger's picture. ("We're sorry. But too bad. He's a public figure.") The paper ran a photograph on the front page of a gaunt, sixty-nine-year-old man recoiling, as if anticipating catastrophe. In that instant, the look in Salinger's eyes was one of such terror that it is a wonder he survived it. "Catcher Caught" the headline screamed in triumph.

On the day Salinger's picture appeared in the *Post*, another novelist of stature, Don DeLillo, began thinking about the inescapable and mystical power of the image in the media age, and, closer to home, about his own half-hearted attempts to keep his distance from the mass-media machinery. From the start, he had been shy of exposure outside the exposure of the work itself. When he published his first novel, *Americana*, in 1971, he had asked that the author's note on the jacket read, simply, "Don DeLillo lives and works in New York City." No offense intended, but he preferred to keep it that way.

After living in the Bronx and Manhattan for many years, DeLillo and his wife, Barbara Bennett, eventually settled a half hour's train ride north of the

131

city, in Westchester County. They live in a green, quiet place lousy with lawyers, doctors, editors, and bankers. They both work at home: DeLillo as a novelist in his upstairs study, Bennett as a landscape designer. (She used to be an executive at Citibank.) DeLillo does not teach, he rarely gives readings, and he keeps interviews to a minimum. When friends would ask his credo, DeLillo would say he lived by the words of Stephen Dedalus: "Silence, exile, cunning—and so on."

But what DeLillo learned from the picture in the *Post* is that the price of complete withdrawal is even greater than the price of media whoredom. Not long after seeing the picture of Salinger, DeLillo began writing *Mao II*, a book with a novelist named Bill Gray at its center. At one point, Gray says, "When a writer doesn't show his face, he becomes a local symptom of God's famous reluctance to appear. . . . People may be intrigued by this figure but they also resent him and mock him and want to dirty him up and watch his face distort in shock and fear when the concealed photographer leaps out of the trees."

There was a time when people who aspired to be a part of something called "the American reading public" felt vaguely obliged to buy, and even read, the fiction of the moment. One felt guilty about missing "A Perfect Day for Bananafish," *The Adventures of Augie March* or *The Group*. There is now more anxiety, probably, about missing *Pulp Fiction* a month after its release than about never reading the latest Saul Bellow novel. Occasionally, a serious novel carries with it a sense of popular urgent appeal and elbows its way past the bilge and onto the best-seller list. The most recent example is Pynchon's *Mason & Dixon*—a phenomenon that may have as much to do with the author's long silence and the exquisite packaging of the book as with the novel itself. Twenty-five years ago, a novel like Philip Roth's *American Pastoral* would have been thought unmissable. No more.

It will be interesting to see what happens with DeLillo's new novel, *Underworld*, to be published next month. DeLillo is sixty, and this, his eleventh book, is his longest, most ambitious, and most complicated novel—and his best. The length is in excess of eight hundred pages; the ambition is to portray the American psyche during its Cold War ascendance, beginning with Bobby Thomson's home run to win the 1951 National League pennant at the Polo Grounds for the New York Giants and ending with an underground explosion on the plains of Kazakhstan after the collapse of the Soviet empire. At the center of the novel is a man named Nick Shay, who, as a teen-ager, shot and killed a waiter in the Bronx; the novel follows Shay, and America, from Thomson's homer, that singular moment of citywide postwar joy, to a jaundiced maturity. Shay grows up to be an executive specializing in the management of waste. Just as DeLillo's 1988 novel, *Libra*, was a kind of fictional biography of Lee Harvey Oswald, *Underworld* also contains imagined public characters, a wealth of them, including J. Edgar Hoover, Frank Sinatra, Jackie Gleason, and Lenny Bruce, as well as Cold War artifacts like a "long-lost" film by Sergei Eisenstein called *Unterwelt*, the subway graffiti and murals of inner-city guerrilla painters, a documentary on the Rolling Stones, satellite photographs, and the play-by-play monologue of the Giants broadcaster Russ Hodges.

In the labelling process that passes for popular criticism, DeLillo has been called "the chief shaman of the paranoid school of American fiction"—and not without reason. Even DeLillo allows that the thread running through his books is about "living in dangerous times," about plots and conspiracies, about troubled men inhabiting small rooms. But, for all the cramped spaces and sweaty foreboding in the novels, *Underworld* included, what's missing from the critical work about DeLillo is the humor, the way the language undercuts, even redeems, the darkness of the landscapes. *Underworld* is the black comedy of the Cold War; it is full of sentences that capture, with the choice of the odd word, a moment in American history. Here is Shay in a contemporary restaurant:

> The waitress brought a chilled fork for my lifestyle salad. Big Sims was eating a cheeseburger with three kinds of cheddar, each described in detail on the menu. There was a crack in the wall from the tremor of the day before and when Sims laughed I saw his mouth cat's-cradled with filaments of gleaming cheese.

Scribner paid nearly a million dollars for *Underworld*, and Scott Rudin, the producer of *Clueless* and *The First Wives' Club*, has bought the movie rights. With a mixture of amusement and resignation, DeLillo has agreed to do his public part, but he has tried to keep things within reason. When he and I first talked on the phone to arrange a meeting at his house, DeLillo said, "I'd ask that you not tell anyone where I live, specifically speaking. You can say Westchester." We met, then, on a summer morning at the agreed-upon hour at the agreed-upon unmentionable train station.

To meet DeLillo, at first, is to meet someone who seems to have sanded away all trace of authorial ego or personal affect: his voice is a flat, wry monotone with just a trace of Bronx; he wears enormous and very thick glasses; his clothes tend toward mail-order jeans, denim work shirts, chinos. His life is equally Dionysian: four hours of writing in the morning, a few miles around a local high-school track at midday ("trees, birds, drizzle"), and then more writing, on into the early evening. Sometimes he will go see a movie. Sometimes he will rent one. DeLillo once said, "A writer takes earnest measures to secure his solitude and then finds endless ways to squander it." He has learned not to squander it much, if at all. When DeLillo started writing, in the mid-sixties, he worked sporadically, and it was only over time that he developed his athlete's focus and rigor, the sense of responsibility, that has allowed him to publish so steadily since *Americana*.

"I didn't become serious about fiction for a long time," he said as we settled into his spare living room. The room is decorated with a few antiques, a few books, some CDs, and fresh flowers. "I didn't have the ambition, the sense of discipline. I had no idea what was demanded of a writer who wanted to be serious about his work, and it took me a long, long time to develop this. It didn't occur to me then that much more was demanded out of me, and much more was at stake in day-to-day work. You know, you become a better writer by getting older, by living longer."

DeLillo did not map out the architecture of *Underworld* and then begin. The process was much more intuitive, mysterious, floundering. There was never an outline. The writing began with a twenty-five-thousand-word burst—a set piece, which became the novel's prologue. It opens with a black kid named Cotter Martin sneaking into the Polo Grounds and then, like a movie camera that widens its focus, takes in the crowd. The opening, which first appeared as a novella called "Pafko at the Wall" in *Harper's*, is one of the most extraordinary performances in contemporary American fiction. DeLillo is able to get the wise-guy interplay among the Hollywood biggies in Leo Durocher's private box (Gleason vomiting on Sinatra's lisle socks), the fears and pleasure of Cotter in his fugitive seat, the animal movements of the crowd, the action on the field, the city's ecstatic reactions beyond, even J. Edgar Hoover surreptitiously studying a small reproduction of a Brueghel painting ("the meatblood colors and massed bodies"). Hoover, sitting in his box, knows that while the game is being played the Soviet Union is secretly testing a nuclear weapon in Kazakhstan, and he thinks, What secret history are they writing? DeLillo's focus, his camera, seems to career around the ballpark, from scene to scene, face to face, mind to mind, taking it all in, as if at once.

After the home run has been hit, he ends the set piece by focussing on Russ Hodges, the broadcaster:

> This is the thing that will pulse in his brain come old age and double vision and dizzy spells—the surge sensation, the leap of people already standing, that bolt of noise and joy when the ball went in. This is the people's history and it has flesh and breath that quicken to the force of this old safe game of ours, and fans at the Polo Grounds today will be able to tell their grandchildren—they'll be the gassy old men leaning into the next century and trying to convince anyone willing to listen, pressing in with medicine breath, that they were here when it happened.
>
> The raincoat drunk is running the bases. They see him round first, his hands paddling the air to keep him from drifting into right field. He approaches second in a burst of coattails and limbs and untied shoelaces and swinging belt. They see he is going to slide and they stop and watch him leave his feet.
>
> All the fragments of the afternoon collect around his airborne form. Shouts, batcracks, full bladders and stray yawns, the sand-grain manyness of things that can't be counted.
>
> It is all falling indelibly into the past.

While the Giants were playing the Dodgers for the '51 pennant, DeLillo was in a dentist's office on Crotona Avenue in the Bronx. He was, naturally, a Yankees fan, so he was mainly waiting it out to see who the next National League victim would be. Thomson's homer was not for him what it was for Giants fans. But forty years later, as he read an anniversary account of the game in the newspaper, he began to think about the event, how it seemed unrepeatable, the communal joy of it married, as it was on the front page of the *Times* in 1951, to the nuclear explosion in Kazakhstan. "Somebody seemed to be wanting to tell me something here," DeLillo said to me.

For a long time, DeLillo has been interested in the passage in John Cheever's journals where he wrote, after attending a ballgame at Shea Stadium, "The task of an American writer is not to describe the misgivings of a woman taken in adultery as she looks out of a window at the rain but to describe 400 people under the lights reaching for a foul ball . . . [or] the faint thunder as 10,000 people, at the bottom of the eighth, head for the exits. The sense of moral judgments embodied in a migratory vastness."

"I had no idea this would be a novel," DeLillo said. "All I wanted to do was write a fictional account of this ballgame, and, for the first time ever, I was writing something whose precise nature I could not gauge. I didn't know whether I was writing a short story, a short novel, or a novel. But I did know that the dimensions of the Polo Grounds were my boundaries. I had no idea that I would go beyond this until after I finished.

"The prologue is written with a sort of super-omniscience. There are sentences that may begin in one part of the ballpark and end in another. I wanted to open up the sentence. They become sort of travel-happy; they travel from one person's mind to another. I did it largely because it was pleasurable. It was baseball itself that provided a kind of freedom that perhaps I hadn't quite experienced before. It was the game."

After the prologue, *Underworld* cuts to 1992 and begins to work backward through the years of the Cold War, so that the day of the game, October 3, 1951, and the day Nick Shay shoots the waiter, are separated by forty years of narrative. The mechanical device that travels through the narrative as it weaves back and forth in time is the baseball—the baseball that Bobby Thomson hit into the seats at the Polo Grounds, the ball that Cotter Martin grabs and takes home, the ball that collectors, Nick Shay included, covet as a talisman of history. The ball is a kind of grail. Many of DeLillo's old themes are in *Underworld*: the increasing power of the image and the media in the modern world; the uncertainty of American life after the Kennedy assassination; a sense of national danger; men and women who live outside the mainstream of ordinary life and language. There is even the whiff, here and there, of that most singular DeLillo trademark: paranoia. But, more often, *Underworld* is a darkly funny satire of postwar language, manner, and obsessions.

DeLillo takes a Nabokovian delight in the American language. Just as the names of American schoolchildren are catalogued in *Lolita* as if they were Homeric ships, DeLillo lists the words of the fifties—"breezeway," "crisper," "sectional," "broadloom," "stacking chairs," "scatter cushions," "storage walls"—and recounts the small tragedy of a housewife at that techno-crazed moment in history: "She'd recently bought a new satellite-shaped vacuum cleaner that she loved to push across the room because it hummed softly and seemed futuristic and hopeful but she was forced to regard it ruefully now, after Sputnik, a clunky object filled with self-remorse."

DeLillo's greatest feat of literary discipline until now was his ability to look away from his native ground, the Fordham section of the Bronx. It is hard to imagine a writer keeping such vivid local colors out of his work for so long.

On a stifling, fly-blown morning this summer, DeLillo led me down Arthur
Avenue, the heart of the Italian Bronx, past grocery stores and pasta joints,
and said, "There was a Mob hit here when I was a kid—a mobster killed
while he was buying fruit. I think it must have been a model for that scene in
'The Godfather' when Mario Puzo has Don Corleone getting shot while he's
buying fruit in the street. He was a mobster from City Island who came here
to shop. There were actually three events like that when I was growing up.
One was the uncle of a kid I knew. And the other was in a liquor store." On
feast days on Arthur Avenue, the women dressed in brown robes and pinned
dollar bills to the plaster flanks of Jesus. On summer nights, the area was
dense with games—stickball, softball, stoopball, bocce—and radios were
playing and the fire hydrant sprayed and on the roof the women yelled down
at the kids for killing the water pressure. Dion and the Belmonts lived up the
street. John Garfield went to P.S. 45 when he was still Julius Garfinkle. The
great Paddy Chayevsky script *Marty* was filmed in the neighborhood, and
when it came out "we felt as if our existence had been justified," DeLillo said.

"I'll show you the old house," he said, and he headed to the corner of
182nd Street and Adams Place. The house is a narrow, three-story place with
patchy asbestos shingles. DeLillo grew up here with his parents, both immigrants from Italy, his sister, his aunt and uncle, and their three kids and his
grandparents. An old man was sitting on the front steps. He had a broad belly
that stretched and belled out the T-shirt he was wearing. It read, "You Idiot,
Your Fly Is Open." Shy and friendly, DeLillo said hello and said he'd lived
here many years ago.

"You wanna again?" the old man said, with a thick southern-Italian accent.
"I sell you a hunnert twenny-five thousand."

DeLillo smiled and said, "See this brick gate? My father built that!"

"A hunnert twenny-five thousand," the man replied.

We were by now sweating, parboiled, but there was nothing much open.
Finally, DeLillo found a pastry and coffee shop that featured working air-
conditioning. After we sat down, I asked him why he'd waited until he had
filled a substantial shelf with novels before turning to the Bronx in his fiction. In *Underworld*, Nick Shay grows up in an apartment building near
DeLillo's old house.

"I needed to wait thirty years before writing about it to do it justice,"
DeLillo said. "I needed this distance. Also, I needed to write about it in a
much larger context. I couldn't write a novel about a background and a place

without putting it into a deeper setting. I plunged into the Bronx in my early stories, but the stories weren't very good. I wouldn't even care to look at them now. They were a kind of literary proletarian story. They were about working-class men under duress. I remember one was about a man who'd been evicted from his house, and he was outside sitting on the sidewalk surrounded by his possessions."

DeLillo went to Cardinal Hayes High School ("where I slept") and to Fordham University ("where I majored in something called 'communication arts'"). His father worked as a payroll clerk at Metropolitan Life, in Manhattan. "You know that Graham Greene book called *England Made Me?* New York made me," DeLillo said. "There's a sensibility, a sense of humor, an approach, a sort of dark approach to things that's part New York, and maybe part growing up Catholic, and that, as far as I'm concerned, is what shapes my work far more than anything I read. I did have some wonderful reading experiences, particularly *Ulysses.* I read it first when I was quite young, and then again when I was about twenty-five. And this was important. I was very taken by the beauty of the language—particularly the first three or four chapters. I can remember reading this book in a part of my room that was usually sunny. It was a very strong experience. But I didn't read as a kid, and certainly no one read to us. This was not part of our tradition. People spoke, and yelled, but there wasn't much reading. I didn't take to nineteenth-century English material at all. It was a great struggle, a great burden, I couldn't concentrate on it. Once, I had to write a paper on a Dickens novel, and Dickens, of course, is easy. I just read the Classic Comics version and managed to get through. It's a struggle to emerge from a place like the Bronx and settle in a place like Manhattan. It represents an enormous journey that involves manners, language, what you wear, almost everything."

Today, Fordham is an easy train ride south for DeLillo, and when he was thinking about the Bronx sections that dominate the last few hundred pages of *Underworld* he would visit the neighborhood: the alleys of the apartment house where Nick Shay grew up, the projects a mile to the south, the cathedral-like Paradise movie theatre on the Grand Concourse, which has since been gutted and left to rot. DeLillo, like any New Yorker, talks about neighborhood in narrow terms. When we passed Bathgate Avenue, he pointed out the street sign and said, "I keep out of there. That's Doctorow's turf." There are still plenty of Italians along the spine of Arthur Avenue, but there are also blacks, Hispanics, Albanians, Bosnians. Walking these streets helped him summon the faces and the mortar of the place, but it also helped him remember the psyche of the times—the way people knew what they knew, the way they so rarely lived in the larger world, except when they took the Third Avenue El downtown into Manhattan and glimpsed other lives through open apartment windows. And since *Underworld* is about the greater world, about the Cold War, his trips helped him remember how he and his neighbors had lived in threatening times.

"In those days, the way you absorbed the news was different," he said over the hiss and gurgle of the espresso machine. "You would have to go to the movies to really see something. There would be a cartoon and a short on the explosion of the hydrogen bomb. It was part of the entertainment, some-how—an extension of the movie."

In 1959, after college, DeLillo moved to a tiny apartment in Murray Hill, the sort of place where the refrigerator is in the bathroom. At first, he had a fulltime job as a copywriter at Ogilvy, Benson & Mather. His friends were other copywriters, funny, sophisticated guys "who were like a combination of Jerry Lewis, Lenny Bruce, and Noël Coward." They went together to the Museum of Modern Art and the Village Vanguard, to the movies that were coming out of Italy and France at the time. In the meantime, DeLillo started work on *Americana*.

It was a tentative start, but after a few years, once DeLillo got a handle on his novel and convinced himself that he was a real writer, he quit Ogilvy, Benson & Mather. To make a little money, he took freelance jobs writing copy for furniture catalogues, dialogue for a cartoon, a script for a television com-mercial. In 1971, *Americana* was published and was pronounced promising, and in 1975 he married Barbara Bennett. They have no children.

"It's a very lucky life for me," DeLillo said. "I've not been distracted by many of the things that other novelists are distracted by. I earn enough money to make a living at it, for one thing. I learned to live very, very cheaply. And family complications have not been a source of difficulty for me, as they are for almost everyone else."

DeLillo's early novels—*Americana*, *End Zone*, *Great Jones Street*, *Ratner's Star*, *Players*, and *Running Dog*—and then the triumphant run of *The Names*, *White Noise*, *Libra*, *Mao II*, and *Underworld*, radiate a sensibility tempered in the sixties and seventies. But, unlike some of his contemporaries and friends, DeLillo has kept mainly to the political sidelines. "I took part in a number of war protests, but only as a sort of marcher in the rear ranks," he said. "I was very interested in rock music. At the same time, I have to say that I didn't buy a single record. I listened to it on the radio. I let the culture wash over me. I used marijuana, not frequently but more or less regularly. I found the sixties extremely interesting, and, at the same time that all this was happening—enormous social disruption—I also felt that there was a curious ennui, a boredom, which actually may be part of my first novel. I think it's something I sensed around me, which would seem to be completely at odds with what you were seeing and hearing in the streets. I suppose what I felt for much of this period was a sense of unbelonging, of not being part of any kind of official system. Not as a form of protest but as a kind of separateness. It was an alienation, but not a political alienation, predominantly. It was more spiritual."

When DeLillo was a young man in the city, he often went to look at the Abstract Expressionists at the Museum of Modern Art. This summer, we met one afternoon at the museum and walked through exhibits featuring the great Soviet poster artists of the twenties, the Stenberg brothers, a series of photographs by Cindy Sherman, and a history of the still-life that began with a Cézanne and ended with a flat white slab covered with milk, the sight of which caused DeLillo's brow to arch. "Nice milk," he said.

Later, over lunch at the museum restaurant, I asked him about the way those museum visits might have influenced his work; how, for that matter, all the excitements of his youth—Joyce, Italian and French movies of the sixties, bebop, and rock music—figured in his novels.

"That's very difficult for me to answer," he said. "But the influence is almost metaphysical. I don't think I could make any kind of direct connection. I think fiction comes from everything you've ever done, and said, and dreamed, and imagined. It comes from everything you've read and haven't read. It comes from all the things that are in the air. At some point, you begin to write sentences and paragraphs that don't sound like other writers'. And for me the crux of the whole matter is language, and the language a writer eventually develops. If you're talking about Hemingway, the Hemingway sentence is what makes Hemingway. It's not the bullfights or the safaris or the wars, it's a clear, direct, and vigorous sentence. It's the simple connective— the word 'and' that strings together the segments of a long Hemingway sentence. The word 'and' is more important to Hemingway's work than Africa or Paris. I think my work comes out of the culture of the world around me. I think that's where my language comes from. That's where my themes come from. I don't think it comes from other people. One's personality and vision are shaped by other writers, by movies, by paintings, by music. But the work itself, you know—sentence by sentence, page by page—it's much too intimate, much too private, to come from anywhere but deep within the writer himself. It comes out of all the time a writer wastes. We stand around, look out the window, walk down the hall, come back to the page, and, in those intervals, something subterranean is forming, a literal dream that comes out of daydreaming. It's too deep to be attributed to clear sources."

I asked DeLillo if he recognized himself when he read academic criticism or journalistic reviews of his work.

"Not really," he said. "What's almost never discussed is what you and I have just been talking about: the language in which a book is framed. And there's a good reason. It's hard to talk about. It's hard to write about. And so one receives a broad analysis of, perhaps, the social issues in one's work but rarely anything about the way the writer gets there."

The most famous political critique of DeLillo came from the right, a barrage that began, in 1985, with Bruce Bawer writing in *The New Criterion* and was then backed up, double-barrelled, in the Washington *Post* by George Will and the paper's book critic, Jonathan Yardley.

In his essay "Don DeLillo's America," Bawer began with the dubious assertion that while one can always find DeLillo's books in stores it is very hard to find some titles by Fitzgerald, Hemingway, or Faulkner. Even more mystifying than the Barnes & Noble angle was Bawer's idea that DeLillo's novels are not believable novels but, rather, "tracts, designed to batter us, again and again, with a single idea: that life in America today is boring, benumbing, dehumanized." He went on, "It's better, DeLillo seems to say in one novel after another, to be a marauding, murderous maniac—and therefore a *human*—than to sit still for America as it is, with its air-conditioners, assembly lines, television sets, supermarkets, synthetic fabrics, and credit cards. At least when you're living a life of primitive violence, you're closer to the mystery at the heart of it all." A novel such as *White Noise*, Bawer wrote, is studded with cheap leftwing "Philosophy McNuggets."

Will, for his part, interrupted his ruminations on the 1988 Presidential race to take offense at *Libra*, a novel speculating on the character and responsibility of Lee Harvey Oswald, as "sandbox existentialism" and "an act of literary vandalism and bad citizenship." He treats DeLillo as if he were a dangerous crackpot, wielding an un-American weapon—a gift for prose. That DeLillo would dare call into question the veracity of the Warren Commission, or that he would speculate about the psychology of a murderer and the culture itself, "traduces an ethic of literature." And that DeLillo would describe the writer as an outsider in that culture is merely a "burst of sophomoric self-dramatization," because, after all, "Henry James, Jane Austen, George Eliot and others were hardly outsiders." Will went on, "DeLillo's notion of the writer outside the mainstream of daily life is so radical" that it "stops just a short step from declaring the writer as kin to Oswald, who, as a defector, was the ultimate outsider." Wow! Don DeLillo as *almost* kin to Lee Harvey Oswald.

"I don't take it seriously, but being called a 'bad citizen' is a compliment to a novelist, at least to my mind," DeLillo said. "That's exactly what we ought to do. We ought to be bad citizens. We ought to, in the sense that we're writing against what power represents, and often what government represents, and what the corporation dictates, and what consumer consciousness has come to mean. In that sense, if we're bad citizens, we're doing our job. Will also said I blamed America for Lee Harvey Oswald. But I don't blame America for Lee Harvey Oswald, I blame America for George Will. I don't think there is any sense in *Libra* in which America is the motive force that sends Oswald up to that sixth-floor window. In fact, Oswald is interesting because he was, at least by his own rights, a strongly political man, who not only defected to the Soviet Union but tried to assassinate the right-wing figure General Walker about seven months before the assassination of President Kennedy. I think in that seven months his life unravelled. I think he lost a grip on his political consciousness, and on almost everything else around him. And I think he became the forerunner of all those soft white young men of the late sixties and early seventies, who went around committing crimes of convenience, shooting at whatever political figure or celebrity happened to drift into range." DeLillo said he didn't pretend to know the answer to the assassination riddle, though he thought there was probably a second gunman. When DeLillo visited the sixth floor of the Texas School Book Depository museum, he wrote in the guestbook, "Still waiting for the man on the grassy knoll."

DeLillo has no idea how *Underworld* will be absorbed into the culture, if at all. He seems not to worry about it. In fact, he doesn't think that the increasingly marginal status of the serious novelist is necessarily awful. By being marginal, he may end up being more significant, more respected, sharper in his observations. Not long ago, DeLillo wrote a letter to his friend the novelist Jonathan Franzen. Franzen is a younger writer, one with great verbal skill and narrative imagination, and DeLillo's letter sounds very much like reassurance to a successor:

> The novel is whatever novelists are doing at a given time. If we're not doing the big social novel fifteen years from now, it'll probably mean our sensibilities have changed in ways that make such work less compelling to us—we won't stop because the market dried up. The writer leads, he doesn't follow. The dynamic lives in the writer's mind, not in the size of the audience. And if the social novel lives, but only barely, surviving in the cracks and ruts of the culture, maybe it will be taken more seriously, as an endangered spectacle. A reduced context but a more intense one. . . . Writing is a form of personal freedom. It frees us from the mass identity we see in the making all around us. In the end, writers will write not to be outlaw heroes of some underculture but mainly to save themselves, to survive as individuals.
>
> P.S. If serious reading dwindles to near nothingness, it will probably mean that the thing we're talking about when we use the word "identity" has reached an end.

In *Libra*, in *Mao II*, and now in *Underworld*, DeLillo has increasingly brought the world of power and celebrity into his work—the world of contemporary history. It's likely that he will continue in that direction.

"I think the press of public events has got stronger in the last several decades," he told me. "It's the power of the media, the power of television. But also, I think, there's something in people that, perhaps, has shifted. People seem to need news, any kind—bad news, sensationalistic news, overwhelming news. It seems to be that news is a narrative of our time. It has almost replaced the novel, replaced discourse between people. It replaced families. It replaced a slower, more carefully assembled way of communicating, a more personal way of communicating. In the fifties, news was a kind of sinuous part of life. It flowed in and out in a sort of ordinary, unremarkable way. And now news has impact, largely because of television news. After the earthquake in San Francisco, they showed one house burning, over and over, so that your TV set became a kind of instrument of apocalypse. This happens repeatedly in those endless videotapes that come to life of a bank robbery, or a shooting, or a beating. They repeat, and it's as though they're speeding up time in some way. I think it's induced an apocalyptic sense in people that has nothing to do with the end of the millennium. And it makes us—it makes us consumers of a certain type. We consume these acts of violence. It's like buying products that in fact are images and they are produced in a massmarket kind of fashion. But it's also real, it's real life. It's as though this were our last experience of nature: seeing a guy with a gun totally separate from choreographed movie violence. It's all that we've got left of nature, in a strange way. But it's all happening on our TV set."

The day we were talking, television was filled with images of the fashion designer Gianni Versace shot dead on the street in Miami Beach. DeLillo was interested not so much in the fallen designer as in the instantaneous packaging of the murder, its sudden appearance on every screen and thus in millions of conversations. "People talk about the killing, but they don't talk about what it does to them, to the way they think, and feel, and fear," he said. "They don't talk about what it creates in a larger sense. The truth is, we don't quite know how to talk about this, I don't believe. Maybe that's why some of us write fiction."

Underworld ends with the fall of the Soviet Union and its conflict with the West. As DeLillo thinks about the era we're living in, and writing about it, he has also been thinking about a passage in Hermann Broch's novel *The Death of Virgil*. "He uses the term 'no longer and not yet,' " DeLillo said. "I think he's referring to the fact that his poet, Virgil, is in a state of delirium, no longer quite alive, and not yet dead. But I think he may also be referring to the interim between paganism and Christianity. And I think of this 'no longer and not yet' in terms of no longer the Cold War and not yet whatever will follow." But six months after finishing *Underworld*, he added, the germ of something really new has not yet shown itself.

On the way to the station to drop me off for the train back from Westchester County to the city, DeLillo said, "What happens in between is I drift, I feel a little aimless. I feel a little stupid, because my mind is at odds. It's not trained on a daily basis to concentrate on something, so I feel a little dumb. Time passes in a completely different way. I can't account for a day, a given day. At the end of a day, I don't know what I did."

Baseball and the Cold War

Kim Echlin / 1997

From *The Ottawa Citizen*, December 28, 1997, p.E5. Reprinted by permission.

Don DeLillo is a writer who has given himself fully to the art of fiction. No teaching. No children. A modest residence outside New York City. Few public appearances.

He is a spare man, in manner and speech. At a rare appearance for the Harbourfront Reading Series in Toronto recently, he acknowledged with restrained politeness enthusiastic whistles and applause from an audience carrying carefully tended first editions of his 11 novels. The reader of Don DeLillo tends to enthusiasm in the original sense of that word, someone "inspired or possessed by the god."

Indeed, the worldview to which Don DeLillo has dedicated his fiction and his life has something omnipotent in it. His most recent novels, *White Noise*, *Libra*, *Mao II* and his new book, *Underworld*, are preoccupied with big questions. History. Time. Identity. He thinks about toxic disasters, the Kennedy assassination, religious cults, rock stars, international political subterfuge, the transience of fame, America's hunger for celebrity. But mostly he thinks about language. His re-creation of American speech rhythms is fresh, sometimes amusing, sometimes heartbreaking, always true. He pushes the range of English. New words. Sentence fragments. Unparalleled dialogue. Sentences that begin in one geography and end in another. He has chosen a symphonic form—the novel—for his serious play with words.

Masterful and confident he strode through varied stylistic ground in the collage he created for his Canadian reading, the prose by turns lyric, comic, dramatic, ironic. But at no time was DeLillo more entertaining than when he read in the speech tones of his native Bronx, a place where the g's are all dropped, where the linguistic dexterity of using f--k in both a street skirmish and a tender flirtation is as necessary a skill as lighting your cigarette from a matchbook with one hand. DeLillo writes, "You need these useless skills to make an impression on the street."

Underworld is a long, complex novel about America during the years of nuclear armament. Martin Amis has called it a "wake for the Cold War."

Its hero, Nick Shay, is a waste management executive who murdered a man as a young street tough in the Bronx. The story unfolds from the 1951 Dodgers-Giants playoff in which Bobby Thomson hit a ninth inning home run off Ralph Branca to win the series. The novel follows the ball, across the stadium and four decades through the hands of the various Americans who want to hold that little bit of baseball history. J. Edgar Hoover is at the game, "a man whose own sequestered heart holds every festering secret in the Western world," and he has just learned of a successful Soviet atomic test.

Waste—human, nuclear, historical, personal—permeates this novel. Waste is buried underground. There are many "unders" in *Underworld*; the undervoice of America, the underdream of history, the underbelly of the Bronx.

Underworld begins: "He speaks in your voice, American, and there's a shine in his eye that's halfway hopeful."

Citizen: In this book there are many words that use "under"—underdream, undervoice . . . Is this the book's centre?
DeLillo: In this book "under" can apply to suppressed or repressed memories or even consciousness. Nick Shay does not want to acknowledge a very strong truth in his life, the fact that his father simply abandoned the family, and he devises an entire mythology about it, a mob hit. Aside from that, I think that all the unders spring originally from my sense of the physical meaning of the word as applied to the burial of nuclear waste. This is when I first hit upon the idea of calling the book *Underworld*. I read a sentence somewhere in Part One about plutonium waste buried somewhere under the Southwest landscape and I thought of the word plutonium. I thought of its source which is Pluto, god of the dead and ruler of the underworld. At first it was just a small revelation but as I kept writing I kept finding myself, as you suggest with this question, treating subterranean realities of one kind or another, physical in the sense of the graffiti writers in the subway, the plutonium in the Southwest, Nick's shooting a man in a basement room and many other instances. The other kind of underworld too, the underhistory of the Cold War, a curious history of waste which forms an underground stream in this book, waste and weapons, and then they merge toward the end. A condom has a sort of life in this book from beginning to end and so does heroin because much of the book is told backwards. We last encounter heroin when the guy Nick shot, George Manza, reveals himself to be a heroin addict. Nick's wife uses heroin in very, very different circumstances. There's a curious kind of cultural

history, mostly informal, of drugs, garbage, condoms. The baseball forms a
kind of underhistory as it bounces from character to character.

Citizen: Does language itself makes these connections, between people,
between different points of time?
DeLillo: Well, that's difficult to talk about because it's difficult to understand.
No one has asked about it. It seems to me that I follow language as it makes
its connections. Language does create a reality that I had not at all planned
on. There's a sense in which I follow language in the way a poet does, openly,
and without immediate concern about precise content, precise meaning. I
have a curious audiovisual sense of language. I now hear a rhythm in my head,
the beat and cadence of sentences, but I also see the letters as they take
shape on the page. I use a little manual typewriter. I see correspondences—
visual correspondences—that strike me, letters in a given word, words in
a given line. Not long ago I realized something about the first sentence in
my first novel, *Americana*, "And then we came to the end of another dull and
lurid year." The words "dull" and "lurid" could just as easily be two other
words, but there is a visual contact between those two words. Lurid is almost
dull spelt backwards, except for the "r." I realize retrospectively that I've been
doing that all along without really knowing it.

I was reading the afterword to Robert Fitzgerald's translation of *The Odyssey*
and he talks about precisely this thing. He is discussing ancient Homeric
words, Greek words, and he talks about the visual correspondence between
words and he calls this the cut or sculpture of words. This is exactly what I've
been experiencing without ever having articulated it. I do think of words as
having a sculptural sense, I always have, and that's why I use a manual typewriter which curiously enough is an Olympia, so I have a connection to the
ancient world, to the gods.

Citizen: There is a scene between Nick Shay and a priest in which the priest
asks Nick to name all the different parts of his shoes—the cuff, the counter,
the welt, the vamp, the aglet, the grommet.
DeLillo: That's entirely part of my own background, a background in which
language was not terribly important. As I got older I began to realize that I
really didn't know the names of things. Other people seemed to. Of course,
there are many common things, everyday things that practically nobody
knows the names of. That's the odd part of it, and that's what the priest,

Father Paul, is talking about. There must be something mysterious and beautiful in the everyday. And there is something curiously elusive about the everyday. But although there was never in my life any scene resembling that, it was nonetheless sort of personal.

Citizen: I was curious about the end of the scene. Nick Shay talks about wanting to know words, say words, and then he says, "This is the only way in the world you can escape the things that made you." Is language escape? From what?

DeLillo: In reading the galleys for this book, and not until then, I noticed that in Part Six, which is the series of chapters set in the Bronx in the 1950s, suddenly there were many less hyphenated words, fused words, words I'd made up myself. The text is suddenly more naturalistic and perhaps more direct and more vigorous, and it occurred to me that in a curious and totally unintentional way in writing this book I was reliving experience and so was Nick Shay.

That is, the language in the book is different in Part Six, in the Bronx episodes, not just the dialogue but the narration itself is different. It's a bit more simple and a bit more direct and more physical I think. That part of the book is filled with people working, garbage men, butchers, women hanging laundry, a seamstress and so on, kids playing in the street, men in the poolroom shooting pool, so if I'm right about this, there is an evolution of the language in the book that directly reflects the evolution of the main character and perhaps of the author. One has found a level of language and of discourse that creates a distance between an individual, a writer in this case, and his background. Not necessarily a distance in a negative sense, but it simply marks a kind of progress out of the old neighbourhood and into the larger world.

When I first started writing I wrote short fiction, short stories set mostly in that particular geography and when I finally got to work on my first novel, *Americana*—the title itself says something—this was a kind of journey into the broader culture. A curious unintentional form of repetition of my own parents' journey, my immigrant parents who came to the U.S. from Italy. This was their way out of a certain narrowness, an economic narrowness, into a country that promised certain things.

When I was in my early 20s maybe that background and those narrow streets seemed to be a bit constricting in terms of what I could get out of them as a writer because I hadn't yet developed a perspective, a maturity as a writer. From this perspective I found nothing but richness, and nothing but warm memories and the best kind of writerly challenge, a challenge to reproduce a specific kind of location and to recount the smallest sort of gesture, and it was a pleasure.

If a reader holds *Underworld* on its side and looks at the cut pages, they will see a book divided by three thin sections marked off with black pages. The effect is one of a fine black skeleton on which hangs the body of the book. The three partitioned chapters recount a heart-twisting story of a day and a night in the life of Manx Martin, a whisky swigger who steals his son's precious pennant-winning baseball and sells it to another man to give it to his son. At the end of this rending three-part sonata Manx Martin sits at his kitchen table, hand burned, conscience only singed, waiting for his son to wake up.

Whatever else *Underworld* is about, things and people disappear and are betrayed. A baseball disappears and a boy is betrayed, twice. A father disappears and a son is betrayed. Plutonium disappears and a land is betrayed. The book turns on loss and reversing the flow of time.

Citizen: The book seems to be structured in two ways, the Manx Martin episodes move forward and the rest of the book moves backwards.
DeLillo: Structure is something I take great pleasure in. In this book the interesting thing is how much of the book moves backwards in a great sweep of time from the '50s in Part Six to the '90s in Part One. But opposed to this is a structural conflict in the Manx Martin chapter. Those black pages are not a proper part of the book that precedes them and the part that follows them. Manx is not part. His chapters come after Chapters One, Three, and Five. He's not part of those chapters, he's different. And then at the end of the last Manx Martin chapter, suddenly these two conflicting streams lock together because on the day after he sells the baseball, Part Six begins. And then the Manx chapter becomes part of the larger chronology of the book.

This is why I write. To try to do things like this.

Citizen: Time disappears and other things disappear in this book. It creates a feeling of ongoing longing . . .
DeLillo: The first mention of longing in this book is on the first page. The kid, Cotter, is getting ready to vault the turnstile, the sentence says, "Longing

on a large scale is what makes history." This is a vast crowd of people carrying in this case a longing simply for victory, for their team to win. It's just a local symptom. Cotter's own longing to see the game is just a micro longing. But as the novel progresses, longings are more intense.

Citizen: You write, "The long ghosts are walking in the halls." Nick Shay has a longing for his disappeared father throughout and the sections about him as an adult are punctuated by a recurring refrain of how he separates his garbage, newspaper from tin from plastic from perishables.
DeLillo: It's a kind of lament that Nick is making. I suppose the repetition, although I certainly didn't explain this to myself while writing this, I just felt it, is a comment on the loss of a certain energy in his life, now that he is a successful and accomplished adult.

And near the end of *Underworld* Nick Shay drives to Tucson to visit his daughter and granddaughter. With his wife he redecorates the house and separates his household waste according to the guidelines. He flies around the world talking about waste management. While reviewing the things he has done, the things he continues to do, he reflects:

> Most of our longings go unfulfilled. This is the word's wistful implication—a desire for something lost or fled or otherwise out of reach . . . We have bookshelves built in the cool room at the back of the house, my mother's old room, and you know how time slips by when you are doing books, arranging and rearranging, the way time goes by untouched, matching and mixing inventively, and then you stand in the room and look.
>
> I'll tell you what I long for, the days of disarray, when I didn't give damn or a fuck or a farthing.

Don DeLillo is 61 years old. He belongs to the American Academy and Institute of Arts and Letters, has won, among other honours, the Award in Literature from the American Academy and Institute of Arts and Letters, the National Book Award, the PEN/Faulkner Award for Fiction. How time slips by when you are doing books. He sees the novel as a "separate entity from writers" and says, "As I was writing this book, I'd like to convince myself that I was performing a personal act of faith in the novel itself. The form itself. People have said in recent years, perhaps for quite a long time, that the novel

may no longer be equal to this crazy, complex spin of the culture that surrounds us. And I say, if not the novel, then what? I think the novel keeps
renewing itself."

He has commented that it took him some time to develop a sense of
the level of dedication that's necessary to do this kind of work. He has also
commented that the secret to being a good writer is to live long. *Underworld*
ends with words on a computer screen, the writer listening to the sound of
small kids playing a made-up game in a neighbour's yard, the word on the
screen extending itself ever outward; ". . . a word that spreads a longing
through the raw sprawl of the city and out across the dreaming bourns and
orchards to the solitary hills.

"Peace."

A word that lives long. Inspired or obsessed by the god, by the word.

Reticent Novelist Talks Baseball, Not Books

David Firestone / 1998

When the ball went over the fence Tuesday night—and there is no longer any need to say which ball or which fence—it shot into a dark utility space, perhaps the only gray area in the whole sunlit spectacle of this year's home-run daydream. Watching it go, feeling the old stirring once again, Don DeLillo briefly hoped the ball was truly lost somewhere in the darkness, perhaps rolling down history's drainpipe into lasting mystery.

"That would have been interesting," he said yesterday, cherishing the mischief of the notion.

But it was not to be, and Mr. DeLillo knows the century too well to believe otherwise. In 1951, the ball that Bobby Thomson hit out of the Polo Grounds disappeared forever into the crowd and lodged in Mr. DeLillo's imagination, becoming a holy relic of memory that appears at significant moments of *Underworld*, his acclaimed cold-war novel of last fall. The ball, quietly changing hands over the decades, winds up on the shelf of the novel's protagonist, who fondles its curves and seams at 4 A.M. to summon the past.

This year's ball, transfigured by Mark McGwire's bat, was marked with an infrared identifying code and immediately retrieved by a groundskeeper for the St. Louis Cardinals, who moments later told a live television audience that he would forgo the memorabilia market and return it to Mr. McGwire and the Hall of Fame. For this generosity, he was quickly invested with the trappings of modern sainthood: a free trip to Disneyworld, a meeting with the President and even an appearance on David Letterman's show.

Mr. DeLillo, whose explorations of America's waste places and dark compulsions have made him one of the country's premier novelists, finds this selflessness laudatory, but believes the neatly packaged moments are finally impoverishing.

"Every baseball carries with it the history of the game, in a mysterious way that you don't find in football or tennis or basketball," he said, speaking

152

as a lifetime Yankee fan who grew up in the Belmont section of the Bronx, his team's home borough. "People have scrambled over baseballs, fought over baseballs, and the wonderful mystery of the Bobby Thomson home-run ball is in part what prompted me to write *Underworld*. If we knew who had that baseball, it's possible I never would have begun work on the novel."

It is mystery that feeds the imagination, and it is mystery, he believes, that is being drained from the public arena, with its multiple camera shots, instant replays and snap moral judgments.

"We want to know everything and we want to show everything," he said. "It's all ultimately a function of technology. In the days of Thomson and Ralph Branca, there was no videotape. The home run could not be shown repeatedly, it could not be exhausted by midnight of the first day. I think that in part accounts for the longevity of that ball game, because it was not consumed so instantly and so readily. The newsreel footage looks like something out of World War I, and there's something precious about this fact."

For this reason, Mr. DeLillo believes that Mr. McGwire's triumph will eventually fade in the public mind faster than Thomson's, blurred by the repetition that he calls "an offense against memory." What may last, however, is Mr. McGwire's gesture across time, reaching back to 1961 with his embrace in the stands of the family of Roger Maris, the Yankee who was the longtime record-holder.

"It was a wonderful gesture," said Mr. DeLillo, who like Mr. McGwire's father is 61 years old. "It was so interesting to see how closely the sons resembled Maris himself. One's memory of Maris is of a haunted face with sunken eyes, perhaps in part because he is still to us a figure in black and white rather than in four colors. I can picture Maris in his Cardinal uniform in color, but as a Yankee, he's permanently part of my black-and-white memory."

The power of memory is one of Mr. DeLillo's great themes, and he talks of it easily, in flowing descriptive sentences with long silences in between, unafraid to be seen thinking carefully before he speaks. Though he dislikes interviews and seemed physically pained by a camera's lens a few inches from his face, he readily agreed to talk about baseball, not as a tired literary metaphor for American life but as a portal that Americans have traditionally used to transcend their lives.

The race to overtake Maris is the "bright side" of the country's obsession with fame and wealth and spectacle, he said, the antidote to the depressing scandalous news from Washington. He has known of this power since his childhood pickup games on the streets of St. Martin's parish, since that day in 1951 when he saw so much of the city kindle in exuberance after Thomson's famous pennant-winning home run. (Actually, he was sitting in his dentist's chair at the time, but he still remembers.)

He lives in Westchester now, working on a play called *Valparaiso* that soon will open in Boston, occasionally dipping into his favorite restaurants on Arthur Avenue and letting himself drift into monochrome.

"I went to Cardinal Hayes High School, which is in very easy walking distance of Yankee Stadium," he said. "I remember one afternoon, in October, hearing a strange sound, a little like surf, and wondering what it was. And later I realized it was the sound made by the crowd at Yankee Stadium when Tommy Henrich hit a late-inning home run. It was against the Dodgers."

"Writing as a Deeper Form of Concentration": An Interview with Don DeLillo

Maria Moss / 1999

From *Sources*, Spring, 1999, pp. 85–97. Reprinted by permission.

Maria Moss is currently Assistant Professor of American Literature at the John F. Kennedy-Institut for North American Studies in Berlin. The interview took place in the "Ermeler Haus," a small hotel near the old (and new) center of Berlin on November 14, 1998. This was one day after DeLillo's reading at the "Tränenpalast" (Palace of Tears; called that way because it was in this rather dreary building that people from the West used to part with their family members and friends from the East).

Moss: If this microphone were pointing at Bill Gray of *Mao II*, would he feel that this is the "aiming of the gun"?
DeLillo: Well, believe it or not, Bill and I have very little in common.

Moss: Thank God! (Laughter)
DeLillo: In fact, even though we're both writers, he was very difficult for me to discover, to find. There's a female character in *Mao II* named Karen, and as soon as I began to create this character, I felt I knew exactly who she was, and it was easy. But it was very difficult—in fact it took me half a book—to even begin to figure Bill out. The fact that he's a writer did not really give me particular access to him. He is an absolutely fictional character. The whole initiative for that book was wondering what would happen if a well-known reclusive individual decided to have his picture taken. That's really what it was. And I simply began to discover what the answer might be.

Moss: This quote seems to fit here. Bill Gray says: "These pictures are an announcement of my dying" when Brita is taking his photos . . .
DeLillo: Very good.

155

Moss: . . . and indeed he does die at the end of the novel.

DeLillo: I think he's in despair as an artist, and I think he has his picture taken because he needs something from which to flee. He needs a deeper level of disappearance. What he's doing now is not enough for him, he has to escape completely. And he escapes into his own dying. That's what happens.

Moss: There seems to exist an ambivalence about pictures and the media in general in some of your novels, for instance in *Americana*, in *Mao II* as well as in your new novel, *Underworld*. You seem to criticize the media while at the same time using different media forms frequently. The title *Underworld* comes from a (fictitious) Sergei Eisenstein picture, for instance.

DeLillo: I am not one of those novelists who feels he is competing with visual media. I don't feel that at all. I love movies, I love looking at photographs. In our culture and everywhere around us we are shaped—to some fairly important degree—by visual imagery: advertising, billboards, television. I think television is a very powerful medium, but I would make a large distinction between television and other forms of imagery, film, for instance, which is an art form. Television is not. And I do make that distinction. Maybe once they have high definition television there could be a new generation of video artists. It occurred to me very recently that my first novel (*Americana*) is about the power of images which I was only vaguely aware of at the time. And there are resemblances between that novel and *Mao II* and, I suppose, *Underworld* also. In *Underworld* there are so many documents, television shows, photographs, movies. I describe entire movies. Why? I felt the need to create a texture of life as we experience it, and I don't think you can do that— particularly not in a novel of this size—without a serious consideration of what we look at. I love movies, and I felt that this novel (*Underworld*) provided a wide enough medium for me to indulge in this feeling.

Moss: Why are you so afraid of images of yourself?

DeLillo: I don't like to have my picture taken when I'm not aware of it. But I'm not hypersensitive. I am just sensitive.

Moss: To come back to images in your novel *Underworld*. There is this image of the nun melting into that of J. Edgar Hoover. What did you want to express with this intergalactic picture at the end of the novel?

DeLillo: What happens between Sister Edgar and J. Edgar Hoover is an illustration of the final word in the novel. There is a reference to the different derivations of the word "Peace." I think in English, if you trace the word back in time, you find that it means a fitting together, a binding together. And that's what I had in mind with Sister Edgar and J. Edgar. They illustrate, I suppose, the idea of peace on a strictly human level. And the idea of that in a novel that's completely devoted to conflict between nations, races, men and women, the idea, a longing at least, for peace might be a way to end the book. And certainly the word "Peace" is not meant ironically, it's meant seriously. But it's all about longing, it's certainly not a realistic expectation. And that's why these two characters merge in cyberspace and become one. And the fact that they have the same name is a curious situation for me. Of course, J. Edgar Hoover had to be called that because that's his name, and I would have been foolish to create a fictional person or to simply change his name. Fiction is not about changing names. Why did I name her Sister Edgar? Well, of course I wanted to make that comparison, but the odd thing is: when I was in Catholic grade school, as a twelve-year-old, my teacher was named Sister Edgar. I was a little concerned about using the real name for legal reasons. But she had to be called Sister Edgar. So I just did it.

Moss: Is the end about redemption?
DeLillo: I think it is, to some degree.

Moss: Did you have the word "Peace"—as your final word—in mind from the very beginning?
DeLillo: No, I thought there would be a different sentence which also occurs toward the end of the book when Sister Edgar thinks she's seeing God, and it turns out to be a hydrogen bomb. The sentence goes: "The jewels roll out of her eyes and she sees God." I thought that would be the end of the novel, and then I realized that that just wasn't right and that's how I ended up with "Peace." I didn't come up with the word "Peace" until my last month or three weeks at work.

Moss: A little before the end there is this scene in which Esmeralda appears in a picture, and one of the nuns says: "Don't look at pictures. Pictures lie." What about the aspect of religion in *Underworld*?
DeLillo: It has happened in the U.S. that people see religious imagery on totally commonplace backgrounds. In Pittsburgh, people were seeing the face of Jesus in a fork full of spaghetti on a huge billboard, and cars would

congregate, and people would congregate. I suppose that this was the sort of inspiration I had for Esmeralda's face being on a billboard, in an orange juice ad. I didn't mean it as some kind of mockery, I meant it as something that happens. Popular culture is inescapable in the U.S. Why not use it?

Moss: Are you a spiritual person?
DeLillo: In a very general sense. I think writing brings me closer to spiritual feelings than anything else. Writing is the final enlightenment.

Moss: What is the role of the writer—the role of literature—in a picture-dominated society?
DeLillo: Fiction has always moved into small, anonymous corners of human experience. The role of the writer doesn't necessarily have anything to do with the visual society at all. It depends on the kind of writer. The interesting thing is that there's a relationship between movies and the novel. They both depend on narrative. As long as there are movies it means that people have a need for the kind of narrative that movies provide. And that's very, very similar to the kind of narrative that novels provide. They are related disciplines. Novelists don't follow, novelists lead. We don't react, at least we shouldn't, to movies or television or anything else. You asked what the role of the novelist is: it's our task to create a climate, to create an environment, not to react to one. We as novelists have to see things before other people see them.

Moss: You seem to have a very romantic image of the writer.
DeLillo: I don't know if it's romantic. I should also add that this is what one says after finishing a piece of work in response to questions about it. It is not really what you're thinking about while you're working. Still, it's legitimate to say these things.

Moss: Does the power of history for you exist only in the 20th century?
DeLillo: Probably.

Moss: So you wouldn't consider writing a historical novel, one that takes place in the 18th or 19th century?
DeLillo: I don't think that's likely. I haven't been there. I would have to do pure research, which I don't want to do. When I wrote *Libra*, I not only looked at all the documents, I also went to three or four or five cities. And that was important.

Moss: Flaubert's or Balzac's novels, for instance, had a dramatic effect on society. Now television and the picture industry seem to have taken over that role.

DeLillo: Certainly, the novel has changed since then, but not because of other media. The novel has changed because *we* have, because our consciousness has changed as a result of wars and other phenomena of the 20th century. Then there was Kafka. I don't know how some contemporary writers can sit down and write what is in effect a 19th century novel, as in fact many successful writers do. I suppose it's just a question of sensibility. Contemporary life has an edge that we didn't know in earlier centuries, and this edge is what defines my work, what shapes my work.

Moss: Why did you choose to write *Underworld* in a reverse chronological order? Why not start with the 50s and then progress chronologically to the 70s?

DeLillo: That's exactly how I started the book. After the prologue ("The Triumph of Death"), Part One originally began the day after the baseball game. I wrote for three weeks about the Bronx of 1951, and I was having a fine time. But I realized there was something unsatisfying. I needed something more radical, I needed a radical leap. That's when I thought I would push—in a flash—forty years into the future and then work back to the ballgame. Once I did this it became absolutely crucial because it provided the structure of the novel. And it was far more interesting to me than simply using a strict, forward chronology. What it allowed me to do was to create a counter chronology, that is, as the book moves backwards over forty years or so there's this character, Manx Martin, trying to save a baseball while moving forward over a period of one life. You can actually see his movement: when you look at the book you'll notice that the black pages create a little stream. Manx Martin is one little chronological stream moving against the huge flow of the river in the rest of the novel. When I did this I began to feel excited. It gave me a nervous impetus. Structure is always interesting to me.

Moss: But why then the fragmented break in the middle of the book? There you're going back and forth over a period of 50, 60, 70 years?

DeLillo: I wanted a departure. I thought there was a certain predictability to what I did. I wanted the 60s in particular to jump back and forth. I wanted them to be frenetic and unpredictable.

Moss: There seems to be a strange sense of nostalgia in your novel. Are you a nostalgic person?

DeLillo: No, absolutely not. If there is this sense of longing, it's not in simple terms. Nick Shay feels a longing at the end of the novel. But it's not for lost innocence, it's for lost guilt. It's for the days when he was able to act, in his muscles and in his blood. When he used to beat people up, when he stole a car. That's what he misses. That's his foremost answer. In general, nostalgia is not something I feel myself.

Moss: Not even for baseball?

DeLillo: There's nothing to feel nostalgic for. The game is still being played. There is something special about the game, yes, and maybe one of the characters in my book, the announcer Russ Hodges, expresses this feeling of baseball's greatness. That's why it is inescapable that the beginning of the book happen at the dawn of the Cold War.

Moss: Do you remember where you were at the time of Bobby Thomson's homerun?

DeLillo: I do remember clearly. I was in a dentist's office, having a tooth filled. The radio was on, and everybody went crazy when he hit the home run. I was a Yankee fan, so I was aloof in a game between the Dodgers and the Giants. Even as a fourteen-year-old I was somewhat condescending toward these two other teams.

Moss: How has baseball changed since then?

DeLillo: It is interesting to compare crucial home runs these days with Bobby Thomson's. By midnight of the first day, you will have seen videotaped replays of important home runs about 82 times. Then they start using the videotaped replays in commercials—with the person's approval, for which he gets paid a great deal of money. The Bobby Thomson home run, in comparison, was hard to locate. It's just old newsreel film, and it wasn't shown very frequently at all. That's the difference.

Moss: In *Underworld* you are describing baseball as some kind of American family ritual. And, of course, in *The Names*, there are the ritual killings by the cult. What is your interest in ritual?

DeLillo: In *The Names* my interest was the way in which a mind centered on ritual can so easily slip off into violence. I thought that ritual stripped from the world becomes dangerous, becomes violent. It loses its connection. It's almost pure silence devolving into nuclear weaponry in a curious way, in the way a theory, a formula on a blackboard, like $E = mc^2$, progresses into a bomb explosion on the other side of the world. It's a little like that. These people had removed themselves from the world. And they were acting out of an impetus of pure mind. I felt this could lead to what it did lead to: ritual killings.

Moss: The novel *Underworld* takes up some of the motifs from your previous novels, the environmental issue from *White Noise*, the focus on different media forms from *Libra* and *Mao II*. Does the extensive reworking of this material imply an exhaustion, or the desire for an exhaustion of these issues?

DeLillo: Not consciously. But in fact, I have moved on to a stage play. And I hope there is another novel following soon. But I understand the question. I don't think that a writer in the middle of his deliberations considers these things, although I suppose that when it's over, one does have moments of self-questioning, like what do I do next?

Moss: In *Underworld*, there are these endless reruns of the Highway Killer scene. What has changed in society with the possibility of constantly replaying events?

DeLillo: Maybe an obliteration of memory has set in. When there is a crime committed in some obscure town in Oklahoma at 2 o'clock in the morning in a convenience store that's open all night, there is a surveillance camera that catches the robber shooting the man behind the counter. It's a murder. And it's a murder that would attract absolutely no attention if it hadn't been caught by a video camera. News stations will then run the video over and over and over, simply because it's there. I think this is the thrust of technology. Once you have the means to expose something, you have to expose it. This is where technology drives the culture in a curious way. I think this is what happened in the Clinton scandal in part. Once the documents were compiled, once the audiotape—the conversation between the two women— was available, they had to tell it, they had to show it, they had to quote it. And that's what they did. They were driven to do it somehow. I think all these repetitions create a warped consumerism. After a while you feel you're a consumer buying violent images.

Moss: The video of the Highway murder in *Underworld* resembles the Zapruder film (the amateur video showing the Kennedy assassination) in *Libra*.
DeLillo: It occurred to me—as I was working on the novel—that there was a scene involving headshots. Even when Nick thinks of his father being kidnapped and killed he thinks of him being shot in the head. Nick shoots a guy in the head. The Texas Highway Killer surely aims for the heads as he's shooting the persons driving the car. I don't know how this happened. I think it has to do with the Kennedy assassination. Somehow this flows through the culture, and it flows through the book. I felt driven to again look at the Zapruder film and to write about it. Writing about it enables me to think more deeply. If I don't write about something, I'm not sure what I think of it. Writing is just a deeper form of concentration.

Moss: Your novels, you once said, couldn't have been written the way they exist without the Kennedy assassination. Are the novels after *Libra* different? Was *Libra* a "coming to terms with," a "purification rite" for you?
DeLillo: I think *Libra* and *Underworld* have something in common. Personally, *Underworld* brought me back into history. After I finished *Libra*—on which I worked for about three years—I began to miss the experience of real events and historical characters, the power they carry, the aura they carry. Just after *Libra* came out, someone else wrote a novel about the assassination. I don't remember the guy's name. It was a "what if" novel. "what if" Oswald had not been killed, "what if" Kennedy had just been maimed. I can't remember all the details. But he changed everybody's name. He changed Oswald's name, he changed Kennedy's name. I felt that was crazy. As I said, fiction is not about changing names. And that's what I missed, the power of history. So when I started working on *Underworld*, it was in a curious way linked in my mind to *Libra*.

Moss: Did you feel that in *Libra* you were exposing a secret part of history?
DeLillo: Well, this is a powerful sentence. I wouldn't put it quite that starkly. In *Libra* there was a specific task I had set myself, which was to fill in the gaps. The Kennedy assassination was an event in which there are missing perceptions. How many shots were fired? I don't think this has been determined beyond doubt. How many shots, how many wounds in the President's body, how many gunmen? I don't think we can know these things for certain. What I

did was provide the missing narrative. This was my challenge: to create the missing seven seconds.

Moss: Did you set yourself a similar task in *Underworld*?
DeLillo: Not so specific, just a novel that covers a significant part of history.

Moss: And of your life?
DeLillo: Yes, my life as well.

Moss: There are writers, like Roth for example, who use their own biography extensively, and there are others who claim that they never use personal experiences in their writings. How important are your own personal experiences for your novels?
DeLillo: Certainly *Underworld* features my own experiences, my own history. Not necessarily in a strict autobiographical way. There's a chapter in the book about an advertising man who owns the baseball. This comes completely from personal memory. But you couldn't call me an autobiographical writer. There are aspects of my experiences in my books, but very rarely in a literal sense.

Moss: There's a scene in *Underworld* in which a small Italian boy comes back from school, handing his parents his report card. When they read it they start crying. I had the feeling that that must have been a scene you personally experienced.
DeLillo: No, I tell you where that comes from. It comes from a poet, an American poet. His parents were looking at his report card and they were crying. He thought he had failed all his tests, but in fact, he got A's, he got the best marks possible. His parents, Italian immigrants, were afraid they were going to lose him, that he would not stay home and be part of the family and help them out as he got older. So they were frightened of a certain intellectual prowess on the kid's part. And I think this is common among immigrant families. But it didn't happen to me.

Moss: A chapter in *Underworld* describes in vivid detail Truman Capote's party. Were you invited?
DeLillo: No, I would have never been invited. I was a nobody. I didn't think of this for many years, but then I found a guest list in an old newspaper article and some photographs in a magazine article.

Moss: And the mask of J. Edgar Hoover?
DeLillo: Fictitious. And he was not present at the party. You can do a lot with one photograph. One photograph can create 20 pages.

Moss: I'd like to talk about the process of writing. How do you come up with situations, how do you invent people?
DeLillo: It's all intuition, it's all feeling, there's no strategy. Essentially, I write what I'm driven to write. In fact, I only make a relatively small number of adjustments as I go along. What I adjust is the sentence itself more than what happens or what people say. I look for the right word or I try to find a word with one more syllable. Before history and before politics there's language, and this is what I mean when I call myself a writer. It's practically all intuition and feeling and impulse and inspiration. *Underworld* was a scene of chaos while I was working on it. I ended up with 17 manuscript boxes, about 300 pages in each box. That was my first draft, and it was all over the room. And there I was at my desk trying to find that word with three syllables instead of four syllables. But that's the way I work. I realized not long ago that the first sentence of my first novel (*Americana*) was: "Then we came to the end of another dull and lurid year." That has a certain cadence, but also there are the words "dull" and "lurid." Almost all the letters in "lurid" are also in "dull." One word is almost the other, a mirror image. I do this all the time, but it's instinctive. Sometimes language just flows. But you got to know when it's flowing the wrong way. That is not so easy sometimes. You think you got something magnificent, and the next morning you look at it and you realize you were a fool. Usually what I have to do is tone things down a little bit. I also have to try to be a bit less epigrammatic. Often my sentences sound as if they were uttered by a French philosopher. I have to be careful.

Moss: In *Underworld* you slide back and forth between fictitious and authentic elements. Why, for example, did you choose the title of a fictitious film ("*Underworld*") as the title for your book?
DeLillo: Actually, the title came first, and then I decided to name the Eisenstein film "Underworld." What I wanted was a Russian presence in the middle of the book, and since this is not a spy novel I couldn't create intrigues. But I wanted something. Why did I choose to do it this way? I really don't know. My inspiration might have happened twenty years earlier when I went to Radio City Music Hall to see Fritz Lang's *Metropolis* with

orchestral accompaniment. I remember it vividly. So I decided to use that experience. About two months ago at the New York film festival there was a show of Eisenstein's *Strike* with orchestral accompaniment. I felt that now my novel was coming out into the world, into three dimensions.

Moss: You once said: "Fiction must contest power."
DeLillo: I don't remember having said it, but I think it's true. Nobody has more freedom than an American writer. But at the same time I think the writer in opposition is an idea that one has to take seriously. The writer opposed—in theory, in general principle—to the state, the corporation and to the endless cycle of consumption and instantaneous waste. In sort of an unconscious way, I think this is why writers, some of us, write long, complicated, challenging novels. As a way of stating our opposition to the requirements of the market.

Moss: Can you explain your success with *Underworld?*
DeLillo: No.

Moss: Do you think it has something to do with the fact that your writing has changed from your other books?
DeLillo: I think it has something to do with that. I think it also has something to do with baseball, at least in the States. More than anything else, however—and this is what I believe, it's the Cold War. The fact that people are just now beginning to think about the end of the Cold War. I think people were ready to read about it. In the States now there is an enormous television documentary of about fifty episodes on the Cold War. Also, more non-fiction books on the Cold War are beginning to appear. So maybe that's why.

Moss: May I ask you a couple of "Hollywood" questions?
DeLillo: Sure.

Moss: Have you received a movie offer for any of your novels? Would you agree to do a movie if you could name a director of your choice?
DeLillo: Hollywood has an enormous appetite for novels. And at any given time there might be three or four or five of my books under option. Which doesn't mean very much, actually. It usually involves a small amount of money. Usually, not always. Then somebody writes a screenplay which I don't really want to read unless someone else tells me it's worthwhile. It's so enormously

difficult to do a movie. Through most of my career the people who have
taken such actions have been young guys who don't have access to enormous
amounts of money. I'm not taking an interest in the movie business, but if I
were to work with a director I respected, that might be a different thing. I
might become involved. Yet, I wouldn't want to write a screenplay. John
Malkovitch was going to direct *Libra*, but then funding just didn't material-
ize. So he adapted the novel for the stage and directed a stageplay in Chicago
which is quite interesting.

Moss: I read that *Underworld* has been sold for $1 million.
DeLillo: That's an enormous exaggeration.

Moss: But it has been sold?
DeLillo: No, it's been optioned. For two years, I think. But I haven't been
involved. There has been a director mentioned, but I don't want to mention
his name.

Moss: Let's get back to *Underworld*?
DeLillo: Yes [quite relieved].

Moss: What did you want to express with the epilogue ("Das Kapital")? Is it
an optimistic view of the end of all our waste problems?
DeLillo: I don't think in terms of optimism or pessimism. I don't know
enough about this to be either an optimist or a pessimist. What I had in
mind was the way in which for forty years we thought in terms of weapons
and failed to think in terms of the waste these weapons produce. At the end
of the novel, a Russian holding company detonates a nuclear device in order
to destroy nuclear waste, a course that such a company—in reality—intended
to follow. If they actually did it or not, I don't know. I didn't see waste as a
subject in fiction. I wanted to write about it because I think it's an important
thing in our lives. It's the kind of thing that's not ignored in the press or by
experts. But I think we tend to ignore it. I don't think we talk about it. It's
curious for that reason.

Moss: Does Nick think of waste as a problem?
DeLillo: Nick thinks like someone educated by Jesuits. Which in fact he was.
That's how I explain the edge that his thinking has. There is this key scene in

the book: he sits in a room with a Jesuit priest, and the priest asks him to name the parts of his shoe. This is important for me. He comes from a background where nobody knows these things, where it's not part of one's education. It tells him what he has to do in order to reshape himself, to become a man of the world. It's all about language. Maybe that's why he very often seems to think like a writer.

Moss: Is this a comment on your writing?
DeLillo: Yes [very emphatically]. I believe it is.

Moss: Could you name people or events that were important for the development of your own language?
DeLillo: I don't know that I can. When I was 20, 25 years old I spent a lot of time listening to Jazz, going to museums, looking at abstract paintings, and watching movies. I think this had more effect—not on the way I write, but on the way I think, on my sensibility—than anything I read, although I was a very avid reader then. I don't know that other people's writings formed or had an impact on me.

Moss: The Cold War is based on fear, and in general, the element of fear seems to be an important aspect in your novels.
DeLillo: When I was working on *White Noise*, I wrote very unconsciously. The novel seemed to make itself up, it seemed to take no effort. I wrote this novel, and all the time I was writing it, I felt a hovering sense of death in the air. I don't know exactly why. Of course, it is a novel about this, but it is mostly a comic novel. I have never been affected quite that way by something I was writing. It was like a cloud hanging over my right shoulder. As soon as I finished, the cloud lifted. I never had an experience like that since. And I don't think of writing novels in terms of fear so much as in terms of self-doubt, which can be a problem.

Moss: You said that Bill Gray and you really don't have that much in common. But the terror you just described reminds me of a statement by Bill in *Mao II*. He says: "Stories have no point if they don't absorb our terror."
DeLillo: One hopes that a story such as *White Noise* absorbs the reader's terror. It gave me terror. But perhaps it absorbs the reader's terror, and that's probably worthwhile.

Moss: Weapons and explosives play a major role in *Underworld*. How important are weapons in the daily life of people? Do you think there is a difference between the States and Europe in terms of people's fear of weapons?

DeLillo: I'll tell you: in the American soul there is a lonely individual standing in a vast landscape. He is either on a horse or driving a car, depending, and either way he's carrying a gun. This is one of the essential images in American mythology.

Moss: Are bombs an extension of firearms?

DeLillo: I don't necessarily think so. Bombs are different. Bombs are a product of the superiority of one's technology.

Moss: How did you feel reading in the "Tränenpalast," the "Palace of Tears," which is in a way a monument of the Cold War?

DeLillo: It was quite an experience. People had been telling me about it before I went. Unfortunately, I couldn't see it very well. But, that's fine. Actually, I prefer reading to darkness.

Unmistakably DeLillo

Mark Feeney / 1999

From *The Boston Globe*, January 24, 1999, p. H1. Reprinted by permission.

"Everything is the interview," a character says in Don DeLillo's play *Valparaiso*, which begins a world premiere engagement this Friday at the American Repertory Theatre's Loeb Drama Center.

Those four words could provide *Valparaiso* with its motto. The play's two acts comprise an endless series of interviews given by its hero, Michael Majeski (played by Will Patton), as he finds himself subjected to a particularly inexplicable 15 minutes of fame after a business trip that was supposed to go to Valparaiso, Ind., instead takes him to Valparaiso, Chile. A more appropriate motto for the play's author might be "Everything isn't the interview." Talking to the press has been almost as alien an experience for DeLillo, the author of 11 novels, as writing for the stage has been. "It seems I do a play every decade," he jokes. His first, *The Engineer of Moonlight* (1979), has never been produced. His second, *The Day Room*, received its world premiere at ART in 1986.

To promote the ART's staging, DeLillo has consented to a limited number of interviews. "I'm trying to develop a spirit of cooperation," he says—not altogether in jest. It's a job he's willing to do, but that it is a job there can be little doubt. Talking to a reporter, DeLillo frequently purses his lips and stares off into space, visibly considering his response. In an era where Oprah is queen and Larry King, interview subjects tend to proceed on automatic pilot (a tendency exploited to fiendish effect in *Valparaiso*). DeLillo, 62, who happily admits to having never done a television interview, keeps his hands on the controls. There are long pauses before he answers—sometimes long pauses during his answers—then the words come in a rush.

He's wearing jeans, flannel shirt, and hiking boots. All that sets him apart from anyone else who might have just come in from the Harvard Square cold—or that could suggest this polite man sitting in a small room overlooking Brattle Street might be the author of such darkling, phosphorescent novels as *Underworld* (1998), *Libra* (1988), and *White Noise* (1985)—are his intense air and epic deadpan. In person, as in print, DeLillo can be very funny, but one would never know it by his expression. The name most often

169

associated with DeLillo on the page is Thomas Pynchon, his fellow master of the paranoid style in American fiction. With DeLillo on the stage, it could be Pirandello, the theater's supreme surrealist. For DeLillo in person, Buster Keaton would be a worthy candidate.

DeLillo's novels are populated by visionary rationalists and buttoned-down madmen, assassins and waste specialists, suicidal rock stars and militaristic football players. No other living writer in English can lend such torque to a simple declarative sentence. "The moment does not whisper the usual things," Michael tells one of his interviewers, in an unmistakably DeLillo statement. Menace and meaning (paranoia's yin and yang) do battle in his books, and technology simultaneously obsesses, horrifies, and beckons him. An interviewer in *Valparaiso* describes flying as "That sort of underbreath of powerful thrilling systems," and that, too, is unmistakably DeLillo.

DeLillo began work on what is now *Valparaiso* in 1991. Dissatisfied with the results, he soon abandoned it for what would turn out to be *Underworld*. The novel took five years to write, and when he was done DeLillo found himself looking at what he'd done on the play. "It seemed, if anything, even more fragmentary and unpromising," he recalls. "But I saw something in it." He went to work and had a finished version within five months.

The theater has long attracted novelists—and usually left them with little to show for it. The most infamous example is Henry James and the debacle of *Guy Domville*. Among contemporaries, one could cite Saul Bellow (*The Last Analysis*), E. L. Doctorow (*Drinks before Dinner*), and John Updike (*Buchanan Dying*), none of whom carved out a second career treading the boards.

The complete control a novelist enjoys over his creation bears little relation to what a playwright experiences. It may be his or her play, but it's the director's, the set designer's, the actors' production. It's the curse of collaboration: Even if the text remains untouched down to the last comma, a playwright's contribution is the necessary, but far from sufficient, condition for a production's success.

For DeLillo, the collaborative nature of the theater is very much a part of what draws him to write for the stage. He's sat in on several rehearsals to take questions from the cast and has had "many discussions" with the production's director, David Wheeler.

"It's exciting," DeLillo says. "I think it's precisely because a novelist lives in a world of fragile autonomy that I welcome the chance to work with other people. It's certainly not something I would want to do exclusively, and for me there is an element in which each form is the antidote to the other."

Collaboration may diminish the writer's authority, but DeLillo is fascinated by the way it can enlarge the play itself. "It's very interesting to rediscover your play through the work of the actors. You can see levels of perception and motivation in a particular character based on the way an actor reads a single line. This is one of the most exciting things about doing a play for me. In effect, the play isn't really written until performances begin. Even then, it's still seeking a kind of self-realization that it will probably never actually accomplish. Of course, that's another major difference between writing novels and writing plays. A play is never quite done somehow. There's no definitive performance."

A lack of definition is central to the experience of the characters in *Valparaiso*. They move in a media miasma, at once cheerful and terrifying, that's all formless form and contentless content. Asked how difficult it was to burlesque something as inherently absurd as talk television, DeLillo (a man of otherwise-unfailing courtesy) bridles slightly.

"I don't consider this parody or satire," he says. "I consider this, really, the story of a man with a missing identity and the means by which he seeks to pursue this identity. It happens that he does it publicly. It's very important to remember that in the series of interviews he does there are technological instruments involved. This, to a certain degree, is also a play about cameras, microphones, and audio recording equipment. This is the taken-for-granted presence of the force of technology in our lives—which I try not to take for granted.

"The drive in technology is always toward somethings that's faster, better, more complete. In this play, there's a sense of complete revelation, complete exposure, and the complete absorption, finally, of the main character. I wonder if there is a secret drive in technology that tends toward a kind of totalitarian perception, something we don't glimpse necessarily. Or whether there's something in us that's brought to realization by technology itself.

"I don't think of this as a play about the media. I think of it as a play about the culture and a particular man who tries to find his self-realization in the public arena. A thousand years ago a man may have wandered into the desert (in our romantic imaginings) and tried to lose his sense of selfhood by becoming a monk in a monastery in some remote region and to try to find a certain transcendence. Here, in this particular context, a man tries to gain a sense of self and he does it by the most public means possible."

The great success of *Underworld*—with everything from a six-figure movie sale to write-ups in such bibles of celebrity culture as *Vanity Fair* and *Elle*—saw DeLillo having his own encounter with the public arena. To what extent might that experience to be seen to inform his treatment of Michael Majeski's unexpected media inundation?

DeLillo dismisses any connection. "The book's reception was an amazing surprise to me," he says, "but nothing in my life changed after *Underworld* except that I got a little mail and more requests, which are things that can be handled in a matter of minutes. The experience did not effect the play."

Still, he adds, "You know, I never thought of this play in terms of *Underworld*. But, in a way, that's about Cold War America, and this play seems to be about the post-Cold War period in which we now find ourselves, a period of personality, celebrity, fame, scandal, enormous wealth, and empty spectacle. There seems to be no difference between substantial news and insubstantial news. And in the play everything melts into something else.

"There's no distinction between public and private," he explains. "Nothing is allowed to remain unseen and nothing is allowed to remain unsaid. There's a tendency of the characters to think of everything as potential footage. Things exist in order to be recorded in one manner or another."

As a character in the play says, "Off-camera lives are unverifiable." Those words are at once a statement of media fact and a presumed source of solace to DeLillo as he gets ready to return to writing fiction. Deadpan or no, there's the faintest hint of a smile when says, "I think at the end of this experience I will probably look forward to being alone in a room again with a piece of paper."

Interview with Don DeLillo

Jody McAuliffe / 2001

Don DeLillo: Do you need to know anything about the provenance of this little playlet?
Jody McAuliffe: Oh, yes.
DD: I wrote it because I was asked to by Robert Brustein for the American Repertory Theatre. It was a benefit event called a One-Minute Play Festival, and I think this was in 1992.

JM: I know you published *The Engineer of Moonlight* in 1979, and that was between publication of *Running Dog* and before you went away for three years and worked on *The Names.*
DD: Yes.

JM: Was this your first foray into playwriting?
DD: Yes, it was, and I'm not quite sure how to explain what brought it about. I think I saw people on a stage, actually, and began to follow them and to listen to them. I would also say that I was aware at the time that I was writing something that probably was not stageworthy, in a way.

JM: In what way, do you think?
DD: Well, I think that play needs a greater thrust than it has, a kind of forward motion. And it's awfully conversational. But I had a surer sense of a piece of theater that seemed a little more stageworthy when I was doing *The Day Room.*

JM: What got you interested in theater in the first place?
DD: Being a New Yorker, I always, even as a kid, was aware of theater, but I never really became fervent about theater the way I did about movies. And that, in fact, is still true.

JM: Do you have a sense of what kind of theater attracts you?
DD: I'm looking at two photographs of Samuel Beckett at the moment. In fact, they're passport photos that somebody sent me. Probably the theater represented by Beckett.

JM: Pinter as well?
DD: I think so.

JM: Do you have any thoughts about your process as a playwright as opposed to the way you work as a novelist?
DD: Yes, it's quite different. When I sit down to work on a stage play, I do so with a much deeper sense of openness. That is, I know that I'm just involved in the first stage of something that isn't going to be realized until it begins to operate three-dimensionally on a stage with living actors. And I don't necessarily explore psychological states the way I do when I'm writing a piece of fiction. I write dialogue. And I don't always feel a sense of predetermination concerning the meaning of this dialogue or the possible interpretations of this dialogue. I feel fairly open about this. And through the rehearsal process. I find it's possible to be enlightened by the ways in which actors render dialogue.

JM: Since *The Day Room* was your first production, was it a strange experience coming from novel-writing, and even playwriting up until that point, to the communal atmosphere of the theater?
DD: It was very strange. I welcomed the communal spirit of the theater. But after the rehearsal period and the previews and the opening, I think I was probably ready to go back into a room all alone and work on a piece of fiction. For me, each form, play and novel, is an antidote to the other.

JM: So you like the balance?
DD: I like the balance. Which doesn't mean I'm going to write one play for every novel, but I do like the balance. For me, another enormous difference is that when you write a novel you have the published book, and that's your novel, for better or worse. When you write a play, the feeling is much more elusive. The script isn't quite the play; the published text isn't quite the play; usually there's no single evening, no single performance, that represents the play in your own mind. So it's ever transient and ever elusive.

JM: How much, if any, rewriting do you do in production?
DD: In production, I would say fairly little. I did make changes in both plays, but not even remotely extensive changes. I do rewrite the dialogue as I'm composing, over and over. Much more than I do when I write fiction.

JM: It's wonderful that you're open to what actors might bring to it even though you do rewrite it so much. Because a lot of times you hear it in a certain way and then it's difficult when actors speak it.
DD: Right.

JM: It can be clashing.
DD: And then there are different productions, which is another aspect of elusiveness. Which production is the one? And I don't know that I've found a definitive answer for that in the case of *The Day Room*, where I saw three productions. An actress in one production was, it seemed, much more skilled than in the other two, but there were other aspects of this production that perhaps were not so expert.

JM: There are so many variables in theater over which we have varying levels of control.
DD: Yes.

JM: Do you have a sense when you have finished the play what kind of an effect you want it to have on any audience?
DD: Not really, no. It's a little mysterious to sit in the audience, particularly when it's the first or second time that the play's being exposed publicly. It might be a preview or one of the early nights of the run. And it's interesting to get a sense of the audience reaction. I don't have an idea of this in advance, and so it can be quite surprising. And what I sensed most recently with *Valparaiso* was a thoughtfulness—

JM: On the part of the audience?
DD: Yes, a sense in which they were very receptive, line by line, to what was being said and what was being conveyed to them. And also, and this was perhaps even more curious, a sense that I'd written quite a strange play, which hadn't occurred to me. It hadn't occurred to me through all the days of rehearsal. It did occur to me in the presence of an audience, because that's what they seemed to be feeling. A sense of the play's strangeness.

JM: What do you begin with? You mentioned with *Engineer* the image of people on a stage. I wondered if with *Valparaiso* that central image of him in the bathroom with the bag over his head was a starting point, or was that something that emerged?

DD: No, that was something that emerged. The starting point was a man getting on a plane and going to the wrong city, a city that had the same name as his destination but turns out to be a totally different place. That was the idea, and it was an idea that I've had for many years. And I'm not sure what compelled me to begin working on it. I started working on *Valparaiso* before I wrote *Underworld* and felt the work was not proceeding satisfactorily. I did, in effect, write the first act, but I wasn't particularly energized by what I'd done, so I just forgot about it. Then when I finished *Underworld* I went back to it. I'm not quite sure why, but I did. And it began to seem a lot more clear to me the second time.

JM: Well, *Valparaiso* is a very compelling variation on that notion that you have in *The Names* where the names of the towns and the initials of the murder victims match up. This is a haunting, mysterious thing.

DD: Right. And in the play everybody pronounces *Valparaiso* the same way even though the three actual cities are pronounced differently. They collapse into each other. Everything in the play sort of melts into everything else. So there's an unreality about the cities themselves. Only the name is real.

JM: You've written a couple of short, but very complete plays, *The Mystery at the Middle of Ordinary Life* and *The Rapture of the Athlete Assumed into Heaven.* I wonder what your thought is about the difference, in terms of your process, between a very short but complete work and a full length?

DD: In a curious way it's harder to write a three-page play than it is to write a one-hundred-and-three-page play.

JM: I would imagine, because it's as if you have to complete a total action except in a very brief amount of time.

DD: The first one, *The Rapture of the Athlete*, came more easily, I think because it's a monologue. But what came first was the image of a victorious tennis player on his knees with his racket raised, I believe, and he's kneeling in blinding light. That's what got me going on that. And in the second case it was a much less describable process—*The Mystery at the Middle of Ordinary*

Life. I don't know quite what got me into it, and what I would say about this little play is that it's a curious fusion of stage play and novel. Of course, it's written in play form, but I think it articulates a question that novelists have asked themselves for a couple of hundred years. Simply, who are the people next door? What do they say to each other? What are they really like? How do they live minute to minute, year to year? And it's that commonplace mystery that attracts a novelist's imagination, and it strikes quite deep.

JM: What's interesting to me about this play is how these people become the people next door of someone else. And they begin their own little cycle at the end. He reflects on this mystery, and they begin to engage in it.
DD: They become the people next door—

JM: Yes, to the other people in the brown house across the way in whom they're so interested. Just as there's a beautiful sense of repetition internally in the text, there's that repetition. It's as if you were in a helicopter and you pulled up and looked down and saw a bunch of houses that all looked the same.
DD: First they're talking about something, and then they become something—

JM: Yes, and then they're doing it. Talking about the tablets and the caplets.
DD: I also realized, curiously, when I looked at the play again, that I lifted a couple of lines from this little play and used them in *Underworld*.

JM: So somehow *Underworld* was already germinating.
DD: There is this kind of a conversation in *Underworld* without the self-referring aspect. The kind of conversation that a novelist might imagine people next door have. And it goes on for four or five pages. This, obviously, was the genesis.

JM: It has a marvelous phrase in it—the notion of something "gradually shattering." Somehow it embodies a weird tension that I think is in the whole little world and little big world that these people live in.
DD: It's a curious thing to write dialogue that you know is going to be enunciated, going to be spoken aloud. And you find yourself fitting together words that have a kind of poetic kinship, more than a kinship based on meaning,

and preferring it that way. Not just because it's going to be spoken out loud, but because it's more interesting. There's something to "gradually shattering." The words are related acoustically.

JM: Yes. And there's a beautiful surprise in it somehow, too.
DD: The dialogue I write for theater sometimes resembles the narrative prose in my fiction. It has a conscious meter and beat.

JM: How does the American theater look from your perspective?
DD: It's harder to get a sense of new writers in theater because the work is being done in many cases two or three thousand miles away. But in film, in many cases, the work becomes available. The New York Film Festival is running right now, and there seem to be half a dozen really good movies by young people. I don't know if you see that in theater so much.

JM: In any case, you don't find that you do yourself?
DD: No.

JM: I don't know. Some people may find that they do, but I don't see a lot that I really like. One of my former students who runs a company in New York says that most of the theater he sees he doesn't like. It's always known as an invalid. Theater is forever dying.
DD: I have a nostalgic feeling for theater even while it's alive and well. It's as though it's an anachronism in a way.

JM: Well, there's something about it, as if it's almost occurring in one of those snow globes.
DD: Theater seems to become more important even as there's less and less of a serious audience.

JM: Do you have a favorite among your plays?
DD: No. I think *Valparaiso* is more adept than *The Day Room*. It has less problems of structure. I don't necessarily prefer it. I think, potentially, if I were to go back to work on the first play, *The Engineer of Moonlight*, it might turn out to be more rewarding than the other two. But I don't know if I'd ever do that.

JM: Why do you think it would be more rewarding?

DD: I think it's because at least potentially it's more deeply rooted in real people and real things. At least that's the way I would have to gear it if I were to work on it again. But the curious thing about my plays is they are not nearly as established in the world around me as my novels are. And that, in my own limited sort of outlook on theater, is an aspect of theater itself. It's not about the force of reality so much as the mysteries of identity and existence.

Index